Also by Edward Hirsch

POETRY

Special Orders (2008)

Lay Back the Darkness (2003)

On Love (1998)

Earthly Measures (1994)

The Night Parade (1989)

Wild Gratitude (1986)

For the Sleepwalkers (1981)

PROSE

Poet's Choice (2006)

*The Demon and the Angel:
Searching for the Source of Artistic Inspiration* (2002)

Responsive Reading (1999)

How to Read a Poem and Fall in Love with Poetry (1999)

EDITOR

The Making of a Sonnet: A Norton Anthology (2008) with Eavan Boland

To a Nightingale: Sonnets and Poems from Sappho to Borges (2007)

Theodore Roethke: Selected Poems (2005)

William Maxwell: Memories and Appreciations (2004)
with Charles Baxter and Michael Collier

Transforming Vision: Writers on Art (1994)

The Living Fire

The Living Fire

NEW AND SELECTED POEMS
1975-2010

EDWARD HIRSCH

 ALFRED A. KNOPF · NEW YORK · 2010

This Is a Borzoi Book Published by Alfred A. Knopf

Copyright © 2010 by Edward Hirsch

All rights reserved. Published in the United States by Alfred A. Knopf,
a division of Random House, Inc., New York, and in Canada by
Random House of Canada Limited, Toronto.

www.aaknopf.com

Knopf, Borzoi Books, and the colophon are registered trademarks of Random House, Inc.

Some poems in this collection originally appeared in the following works:
For the Sleepwalkers, *copyright © 1981 by Edward Hirsch (Alfred A. Knopf)*
Wild Gratitude, *copyright © 1985 by Edward Hirsch (Alfred A. Knopf)*
The Night Parade, *copyright © 1989 by Edward Hirsch (Alfred A. Knopf)*
Earthly Measures, *copyright © 1994 by Edward Hirsch (Alfred A. Knopf)*
On Love, *copyright © 1998 by Edward Hirsch (Alfred A. Knopf)*
Lay Back the Darkness, *copyright © 2003 by Edward Hirsch (Alfred A. Knopf)*
Special Orders, *copyright © 2008 by Edward Hirsch (Alfred A. Knopf)*

Library of Congress Cataloging-in-Publication Data
Hirsch, Edward.
The living fire: new and selected poems (1975–2010) / by Edward Hirsch—1st ed.

p.   cm
ISBN 978-0-375-41522-7
I. Title.
PS3558.164L58 2010
811'.54—dc22   2009024452

Manufactured in the United States of America

First Edition

For Lauren Watel

Contents

New Poems

From *For the Sleepwalkers* (1981)

From *Wild Gratitude* (1986)

From *Lay Back the Darkness* (2003)

From *Special Orders* (2008)

New Poems

The Beginning of Poetry

Railroad tracks split the campus in half
and at night you'd lie on your narrow cot
and listen to the lonely whistle
of a train crossing the prairie in the dark.

On the Anniversary of Joseph Brodsky's Death

JANUARY 2001

Archangelsk, the briny cold, the frigid Baltics,
Children throwing snowballs at Soviet statues.

The Arctic chill of the moon at midday,
The trees wrapped, the pedestrians bundled.

How the sun shivered behind the smokestacks
Like a soldier frozen in place.

At the dimly lit Museum of the Far North
The subject was the poet's internal exile,

Metaphysics versus History, and the fateful
Struggle between Poetry and Time,

A Cold War that will never end.
Also, his love for watery ports

And stubborn cats, especially the Russian
Blue that hailed from the White Sea.

Afterwards, a slushy walk, salty air,
Sleep in an overcoat in a converted barracks.

All night I heard the muffled boots
Of an army marching through the streets

Under the thick cover of darkness.
But in the morning, anniversary mourning,

I woke to a magisterial silence.
Snow occupied the city.

Isis Unveiled

The Indian café and the occult bookstore
that had been forgotten by time,
which is immaterial, are gone,

and so are the endless rainy afternoons
when I sat reading—or trying to read—
the mystical tracts of the Golden Dawn

that so inspired Yeats and Maud Gonne,
while a cranky one-armed waiter
played chess by himself in the corner.

I sipped steaming cups of spiced tea
and despaired over the leaden prose
of a system I couldn't crack,

Isis hidden behind too many veils
and Reality fogged like the city itself.
Even the windows seemed Rosicrucian.

Outside, the side streets were crooked
fingers, indexes pointing nowhere,
tucked in sleeves, dead-ends.

The Indian café and the occult bookstore
and the dreamy skeptic I was
are inside me still, and so is the night

I carried my books through a labyrinth
of mysterious buildings, obscure signs,
and ended up on the edge of a vast park

where the sky suddenly brightened
overhead, a west wind lifted
the wet leaves from the wet ground

and trees shimmered in the distance
like the airy shades of women
dancing in black slips.

Winter in Edinburgh

We were far away from the Festival
and the Fringe in our stone tenement.
And we were far from the Enlightenment
in our dimly lit casino, *The Firth of Forth,*
that bobbed like a boat on the North Sea.

But I was glad to be sipping Scotch
in the corner with Irene, the blackjack dealer,
who was married to a mechanic,
while the roulette wheel stuttered and stopped
and my roommates punted away their salaries.

And I was always a little chilled and drunk
when she showed up after her shift
to teach me something about the body,
to shudder down on me from a tower
and sleep on my chest, like a thistle.

Dark Tour

1. *Concord*

A discordant day
in the library leafing
through an old atlas.

2. *Helsinki*

My love, let me know
when you find one person in
accord with himself.

3. *Copenhagen*

In the lion's den
of our bed, I could not cope
with your rude remark.

4. *Stockholm*

Epic domestic:
our stock was down and our home
was always mortgaged.

5. *Dresden*

Compromised city,
lie and lie again on both
banks of the river.

6. Warsaw

Then we sawed away
at the iron pact we made
to stay together.

7. Budapest

No sign of Buddha,
but a history of pest-
ilence and beauty.

8. Delphi

We traveled for days
but the oracle was closed
for the likes of us.

9. Pompeii

As we pompously
quarreled amidst the ruins,
someone stole your purse.

10. Rome

In a Roman bath,
old aroma therapy.
Time for a new age.

11. *Madrid*

Mad at each other
in a romantic city.
Love got rid of us.

12. *Amsterdam*

Unlike the city,
we were a dam that broke up
over the Amstel.

13. *London*

bridge is falling down,
falling down (it was a game)—
and then we fell, too.

14. *Prague*

Try to remember:
we were still bohemians;
the split was peaceful.

15. *Split*

Once upon a time,
children, there was a kingdom:
Yugoslavia.

16. *Barcelona*

Alone in a bar,
I was a Gaudí building
gaudily melting.

17. *Paris*

Everyone in pairs.
My darkness constellated
the City of Light.

18. *Belfast*

Let the bells quicken.
We've lived through enough troubles
for a few lifetimes.

19. *Turin*

The fog ascended,
a shroud above the city.
Our dark tour lightened.

20. *Bucharest*

The accordion
squeezed us together again
in Little Paris.

21. *Milan*

Books were in style.
Love was in fashion again.
You could still read me.

22. *Vienna*

We felt so lucky
that we crossed all twelve bridges
over the Danube.

23. *Athens*

Goddess Athena,
we offered an olive branch
and you brought us peace.

24. *St. Petersburg*

It never darkened.
You shimmied out of your dress
in the gondola.

25. *Berlin*

Athens on a spree.
The wall collapsed between us.
East coupled with West.

26. *Geneva*

We reached an accord
and deemed our sex by the lake
"unconventional."

27. *Lucerne*

Two things startled me:
the mountains over the lake,
your body at dawn.

28. *Corfu*

We slept on the sand
where a man and a woman
can be an island.

29. *Salzburg*

Chords of music, chords
of light in the salt castle.
Unexpected joy.

30. *Concord*

Sunlight in the trees.
A day in the woods leafing
a fresh concordance.

Once, in Helsinki

Once, in Helsinki,
I walked to the edge of town
    in blanketing snow.

It was a whiteout,
an epic storyteller
    without a story,

with nothing to say
about the onrushing cold
    and the blinding day.

All I had to do
was turn around and go home
    to my darkened room

in the youth hostel,
but I stood there mesmerized
    by the frozen light.

Hell was sinking in.
I was alone in a world
    without a vision.

The Case Against Poetry

While you made the case against poetry—
Plato's critique of the irrational,
Homeric lying, deluded citizens—
to a group of poets in Prague,

night deepened in old windows,
swallows gathered on a narrow ledge
and called to the vanishing twilight,
and a beggar began to sing in the street.

Early Sunday Morning

I used to mock my father and his chums
for getting up early on Sunday morning
and drinking coffee at a local spot,
but now I'm one of those chumps.

No one cares about my old humiliations,
but they go on dragging through my sleep
like a string of empty tin cans rattling
behind an abandoned car.

It's like this: just when you think
you have forgotten that red-haired girl
who left you stranded in a parking lot
forty years ago, you wake up

early enough to see her disappearing
around the corner of your dream
on someone else's motorcycle,
roaring onto the highway at sunrise.

And so now I'm sitting in a dimly lit
café full of early-morning risers,
where the windows are covered with soot
and the coffee is warm and bitter.

Anything but Standard

It was the two of us, wasn't it, on those steamy nights
circling the low-slung museum across the street
and lingering by the pond behind the chapel.

It's how the southern clouds passed slowly
overhead, season after season, year after year,

as you followed a low intricate scent
across the stately lit lawn,
and studied the squirrels in the live oaks,
and waded into the brown reflecting pool
with the broken obelisk.

You were a descendent of water dogs
and anything but standard
when you materialized out of the sticky heat
with your dripping black forehead
and delinquent grin, a growl unmuzzled.

It was your Russian face that steadied me
as I sat on a battered wooden bench,
lost in a night that wouldn't end,
and you lay down—calm, poised, watchful—
and stirred beside me on the simmering grass.

Let's get up and go.
Trot ahead of me, old friend,
and shake off the watery darkness.

Milk

My mother wouldn't be cowed into nursing
and decided that formula was healthier
than the liquid from her breasts.

And so I never sucked a single drop
from the source, a river dried up.
It was always bottled for me.

But one night in my mid-thirties
in a mirrored room off Highway 59
a woman who had a baby daughter

turned to me with an enigmatic smile
and cupped my face in her chapped hands
and tipped her nipple into my mouth.

This happened a long time ago in another city
and it is wrong to tell about it.
It was infantile to bring it up in therapy.

And yet it is one of those moments—
misplaced, involuntary—that swim up
out of the past without a conscience:

She lifts my face and I taste it—
the sudden spurting nectar,
the incurable sweetness that is life.

Last Saturday

Then the doorbell rang suddenly,
like an alarm, on Saturday morning.
"Who's there?" I called out.
"The new exterminator."

I was infested, it's true,
but I never expected him to come
so early, without warning.
I never expected him to be so young.

Forebodings

These ravens gathering on the beach
in the battered blue light of dusk
are a sudden unkindness

The path heading up to the house
strays off into a vague straggle
like a thought that has gone too far

That sliver peering through the clouds
looks like a bell that can no longer ring
in an abandoned church steeple

I don't mind the mindless fog
but my room at the top of the stairs
tilts like a broken boat at sea

All night I feel the homesick waves
and hear ravens scavenging in my sleep

What the Last Evening
Will Be Like

You're sitting at a small bay window
in an empty café by the sea.
It's nightfall, and the owner is locking up,
though you're still hunched over the radiator,
which is slowly losing warmth.

Now you're walking down to the shore
to watch the last blues fading on the waves.
You've lived in small houses, tight spaces—
the walls around you kept closing in—
but the sea and the sky were also yours.

No one else is around to drink with you
from the watery fog, shadowy depths.
You're alone with the whirling cosmos.
Goodbye, love, far away, in a warm place.
Night is endless here, silence infinite.

From

For the Sleepwalkers

(1981)

Song Against Natural Selection

The weak survive!
A man with a damaged arm,
a house missing a single brick, one step
torn away from the other steps
the way I was once torn away
from you; this hurts us, it

isn't what we'd imagined, what
we'd hoped for when we were young
and still hoping for, still imagining things,
but we manage, we survive. Sure,
losing is hard work, one limb severed
at a time makes it that much harder

to get around the city, another word
dropped from our vocabularies
and the remaining words are that much heavier
on our tongues, that much further
from ourselves, and yet people
go on talking, speech survives.

It isn't easy giving up limbs,
trying to manage with that much
less to eat each week, that much more
money we know we'll never make,
things we not only can't buy, but
can't afford to look at in the stores;

this hurts us, and yet we manage, we survive
so that losing itself becomes a kind
of song, our song, our only witness
to the way we die, one day at a time;
a leg severed, a word buried; this
is how we recognize ourselves, and why.

Dusk

The sun is going down tonight
like a wounded stag staggering through the brush
with an enormous spike in its heart
and a single moan in its lungs. There

is a light the color of tarnished metal
galloping at its side, and fresh blood
is steaming through its throat. Listen!
The waves, too, sound like the plunging

of hooves, or a wild hart simply
crumpling on the ground. I imagine
there are hunters beating through the woods
with their scythes and their tired dogs

chasing the wounded scent, and I suppose
there are mothers crying out for their children
in the fog. Because it is dusk. Yes,
dusk with its desperate colors of erasure,

its secrets of renunciation, and its long
nightmares beyond. And now here is the night
with its false promise of sleep, its wind
leafing through the grass, its vacant

spaces between stars, its endless memory
of a world going down like a stag.

Insomnia

Undressing the cold body
you lie down at dusk, blue shine

on the windows and the sun
husked for winter night. Tight-lipped

and longing to embody sleep,
to devour the white lion

sleep, you watch the room slowly
steep itself in shadows, steep

itself in the wine-flushed darkness
of another night. Silently

you confront the blue-rimmed edge
of outer dark, those crossroads

where we meet the dead, knowing
their first street calls will rise

and nuzzle against your chest
like tiny inexorable animals

or the blunt edge of a knife
about to descend. And all night

you're left sitting at a desk
frightened, thinking of the skull

under the smooth skin, how we
return to our lives as animals

engulfed in soft fog, exposed
to the wind against our fur

and denied warmth, denied rest,
denied earth's sleep and granite.

How to Get Back to Chester

I remember the greasy moon floating
like a tire over the highway, the last
stars flecked like dust on the window
of my father's garage. For years I've walked
away from the concrete fields of a lousy
childhood, the damp haze of life in Chester,

but now I've come back to follow the
moon through the toothed stacks of chimneys,
through the back alleys lit up by shabby
yellow lanterns. I've come here to stand
like a pilgrim before the tin shacks
holding their tin ears on the highway

while trucks roar by without stopping
and factories clack their fat tongues
together in wind. I've come here to listen
to strangers talk about football, to waitresses
talk about strangers. I've come to see myself
taking the deep blasts from an old furnace.

Not much has changed here, and yet
not much is left of childhood, either.
If you want to get back to Chester
you have to listen; you have to stand
like a penitent in your bare feet
and feel the air darken before a storm;

you have to stare at the one viny
plant waving on the family porch
until you feel your father's grimy palm
gripping your hand, until you finally taste
the words at the back of your own mouth, saying
Don't come back, son. And welcome.

For the Sleepwalkers

Tonight I want to say something wonderful
for the sleepwalkers who have so much faith
in their legs, so much faith in the invisible

arrow carved into the carpet, the worn path
that leads to the stairs instead of the window,
the gaping doorway instead of the seamless mirror.

I love the way that sleepwalkers are willing
to step out of their bodies into the night,
to raise their arms and welcome the darkness,

palming the blank spaces, touching everything.
Always they return home safely, like blind men
who know it is morning by feeling shadows.

And always they wake up as themselves again.
That's why I want to say something astonishing
like: *Our hearts are leaving our bodies.*

Our hearts are thirsty black handkerchiefs
flying through the trees at night, soaking up
the darkest beams of moonlight, the music

of owls, the motion of wind-torn branches.
And now our hearts are thick black fists
flying back to the glove of our chests.

We have to learn to trust our hearts like that.
We have to learn the desperate faith of sleep-
walkers who rise out of their calm beds

and walk through the skin of another life.
We have to drink the stupefying cup of darkness
and wake up to ourselves, nourished and surprised.

Still Life: An Argument

Listen, it only takes a moment
to move, to knot ourselves
together like the ends of a rope
longing to be knotted together,

but let's avoid it, let's wait.
Ropes, even the sturdiest ropes,
pull, they strain, struggle, eventually
they break. But think of it;

in a still life a knife
pauses above a platter of
meat, it only takes a second, and
poof it becomes the idea of a knife,

the drawing of a knife suspended
in the air like a guillotine
about to weightlessly drop on the
neck of a murderer and send him

shrieking into oblivion forever,
but it never happens, the knife
keeps falling and falling, but never
falls. That knife could be us.

The milk on the table is always
about to spill, the meat could be
encased in wax paper to be
protected from flies, but it's

not, it's unnecessary, the flies
threaten to descend on the
exposed meat, but they can't, they're
no longer flies, but a painting of flies,

the blood pooled on the platter
of meat never evaporates, it can't;
look, it's still there; and if I
never touch you, well then, we never die.

Listen, even lovers have still lives,
have whole months when they hang
together like moths on an unlit
light bulb, waiting for the bulb to light,

but if it never does then the moths
survive, meat should be allowed
to sit on the table forever
without being devoured by flies

and if that's not possible, well
then we still have this picture,
the still life not of how it will be,
but of how it was, for the knife and the meat

and the flies, and for us the night we
hesitated together. From now on, love,
we will always be about to destroy
each other, always about to touch.

Song

This is a song for the speechless,
the dumb, the mute and the motley,
the unmourned! This is a song for every
pig that was too thin to be slaughtered
last night, but was slaughtered
anyway, every worm that was hooked
on a hook that it didn't expect,
every chair in New York City that has
no arms or legs, and can't speak English,
every sofa that has ever been torn
apart by the children or the dog
and earmarked for the dump, every sheet
that was lost in the laundry, every
car that has been stripped down and
abandoned, too poor to be towed away,
too weak and humble to protest.
Listen, this song is for you even if
you can't listen to it, or join in;
even if you don't have lungs, even
if you don't know what a song is,
or want to know. This song is for
everyone who is not listening tonight
and refuses to sing. Not singing
is also an act of devotion; those
who have no voices have one tongue.

A Chinese Vase

Sometimes I think that my body is a vase
With me in it, a blue-tiled Chinese vase

That I return to, sometimes, in the rain.
It's raining hard, but inside the little china vase

There is clean white water circling slowly
Through the shadows like a flock of yellow geese

Circling over a small lake, or like the lake itself
Ruffled with wind and geese in a light rain

That is not dirty, or stained, or even ruffled by
The medley of motors and oars and sometimes even sails

That are washed each summer to her knees. It's raining
In the deep poplars and in the stand of gray pines;

It's snowing in the mountains, in the Urals, in the
Wastes of Russia that have edged off into China;

The rain has turned to sleet and the sleet
Has turned to snow in the sullen black clouds

That have surfaced in the cracks of that Chinese
Vase, in the wrinkles that have widened like rivers

In that vase of china. It's snowing harder and harder
Now over the mountains, but inside the mountains

There is a sunlit cave, a small cave, perhaps,
Like a monk's cell, or like a small pond

With geese and with clear mountain water inside.
Sometimes I think that I come back to my body

The way a penitent or a pilgrim or a poet
Or a whore or a murderer or a very young girl

Comes for the first time to a holy place
To kneel down, to forget the impossible weight

Of being human, to drink clear water.

The River Merchant:
A Letter Home

Sometimes the world seems so large,
You have no idea. Out here at dusk
The barges pull the heaviest cargo, sometimes
They drag whole ships to the sea. Imagine
The sound of geese shrieking everywhere,
More geese than you can imagine,
Clustered together and flapping like stars.
Sometimes there are two moons shining at
Once, one clouded in the treetops, one
Breaking into shadows on the river.
I don't know what this means.

But from the hill's brow I can see
The lights in every village flickering on,
One by one, but slowly, like this,
Until the whole world gleams
Like small coins. Believe me:
There are so many villages like ours,
So many lights all gleaming together
But all separate too, like those moons.
It is too much. I am older now.
I want to return to that fateful place
Where the river narrows toward home.

Transfigured Night, Come Down to Me, Slowly

I am walking through the cemetery one more time
waiting for the night-blooming cereus to bloom
once more, on its own, in the dark. I am
listening to the serious wind ruffle the broad
chest of grass, the tired muscles of earth,
the scrawny roots that reach into the mud
like a blistered foot, or a bony hand.
I am watching a cluster of green fists shine
on the bough of a pear tree like enormous
gray moths, or a string of tiny lamps.

Transfigured night, come down to me, slowly.
Bring me your wind and your stars, bring me
a yellow wing brushed against my eyes,
a clear window of moonlight that shatters
once more, on its own, yes, in the dark.
By now the old griefs have hardened
In my chest like a thick chunk of fat.
By now my hands have swollen into fists.
I want to hear the dead lips moving.
I want to feel the thumbprint of another life.

From

Wild Gratitude

(1986)

I Need Help

For all the insomniacs in the world
I want to build a new kind of machine
For flying out of the body at night.
This will win peace prizes, I know it,
But I can't do it myself; I'm exhausted,
I need help from the inventors.

I admit I'm desperate, I know
That the legs in my legs are trembling
And the skeleton wants out of my body
Because the night of the rock has fallen.
I want someone to lower a huge pulley
And hoist it back over the mountain

Because I can't do it alone. It is
So dark out here that I'm staggering
Down the street like a drunk or a cripple;
I'm almost a hunchback from trying to hold up
The sky by myself. The clouds are enormous
And I need strength from the weight lifters.

How many nights can I go on like this
Without a single light from the sky: no moon,
No stars, not even one dingy street lamp?
I want to hold a rummage sale for the clouds
And send up flashlights, matchbooks, kerosene,
And old lanterns. I need bright, fiery donations.

And how many nights can I go on walking
Through the garden like a ghost listening
To flowers gasping in the dirt—small mouths
Gulping for air like tiny black asthmatics
Fighting their bodies, eating the wind?
I need the green thumbs of a gardener.

And I need help from the judges. Tonight
I want to court-martial the dark faces
That flare up under the heavy grasses—
So many blank moons, so many dead mouths
Holding their breath in the shallow ground,
Almost breathing. I have no idea why

My own face is never among them, but
I want to stop blaming myself for this,
I want to hear the hard gavel in my chest
Pounding the verdict, "Not guilty as charged,"
But I can't do this alone, I need help
From the serious men in black robes.

And because I can't lift the enormous weight
Of this enormous night from my shoulders
I need help from the six pallbearers of sleep
Who rise out of the slow, vacant shadows
To hoist the body into an empty coffin.
I need their help to fly out of myself.

Fall

Fall, falling, fallen. That's the way the season
Changes its tense in the long-haired maples
That dot the road; the veiny hand-shaped leaves
Redden on their branches (in a fiery competition
With the final remaining cardinals) and then
Begin to sidle and float through the air, at last
Settling into colorful layers carpeting the ground.
At twilight the light, too, is layered in the trees
In a season of odd, dusky congruences   a scarlet tanager
And the odor of burning leaves, a golden retriever
Loping down the center of a wide street and the sun
Setting behind smoke-filled trees in the distance,
A gap opening up in the treetops and a bruised cloud
Blamelessly filling the space with purples. Everything
Changes and moves in the split second between summer's
Sprawling past and winter's hard revision, one moment
Pulling out of the station according to schedule,
Another moment arriving on the next platform. It
Happens almost like clockwork: the leaves drift away
From their branches and gather slowly at our feet,
Sliding over our ankles, and the season begins moving
Around us even as its colorful weather moves us,
Even as it pulls us into its dusty, twilit pockets.
And every year there is a brief, startling moment

When we pause in the middle of a long walk home and
Suddenly feel something invisible and weightless
Touching our shoulders, sweeping down from the air:
It is the autumn wind pressing against our bodies;
It is the changing light of fall falling on us.

Omen

I lie down on my side in the moist grass
And drift into a fitful half-sleep, listening
To the hushed sound of wind in the trees.

The moon comes out to stare—glassy, one-eyed—
But then turns away from the ground, smudged.
It's October, and the nights are getting cold:

The sky is tinged with purple, speckled red.
The clouds gather like an omen above the house
And I can't stop thinking about my closest friend

Suffering from cancer in a small, airless ward
In a hospital downtown. At 37 he looks
Boyish and hunted, fingered by illness, scared.

When I was a boy the summer nights were immense—
Clear as a country lake, pure, bottomless.
The stars were like giant kites, casting loose . . .

The fall nights were different—schoolbound, close—
With too many stormy clouds, too many rules.
The rain was a hammer banging against the house,

Beating against my head. Sometimes I'd wake up
In the middle of a cruel dream, coughing
And lost, unable to breathe in my sleep.

My friend says the pain is like a mule
Kicking him in the chest, again and again,
Until nothing else but the pain seems real.

Tonight the wind whispers a secret to the trees,
Something stark and unsettling, something terrible
Since the yard begins to tremble, shedding leaves.

I know that my closest friend is going to die
And I can feel the dark sky tilting on one wing,
Shuddering with rain, coming down around me.

Fast Break

—In Memory of Dennis Turner, 1946–1984

A hook shot kisses the rim and
hangs there, helplessly, but doesn't drop,

and for once our gangly starting center
boxes out his man and times his jump

perfectly, gathering the orange leather
from the air like a cherished possession

and spinning around to throw a strike
to the outlet who is already shoveling

an underhand pass toward the other guard
scissoring past a flat-footed defender

who looks stunned and nailed to the floor
in the wrong direction, trying to catch sight

of a high, gliding dribble and a man
letting the play develop in front of him

in slow motion, almost exactly
like a coach's drawing on the blackboard,

both forwards racing down the court
the way that forwards should, fanning out

and filling the lanes in tandem, moving
together as brothers passing the ball

between them without a dribble, without
a single bounce hitting the hardwood

until the guard finally lunges out
and commits to the wrong man

while the power-forward explodes past them
in a fury, taking the ball into the air

by himself now and laying it gently
against the glass for a lay-up,

but losing his balance in the process,
inexplicably falling, hitting the floor

with a wild, headlong motion
for the game he loved like a country

and swiveling back to see an orange blur
floating perfectly through the net.

Edward Hopper and
the House by the Railroad (1925)

Out here in the exact middle of the day,
This strange, gawky house has the expression
Of someone being stared at, someone holding
His breath underwater, hushed and expectant;

This house is ashamed of itself, ashamed
Of its fantastic mansard rooftop
And its pseudo-Gothic porch, ashamed
Of its shoulders and large, awkward hands.

But the man behind the easel is relentless;
He is as brutal as sunlight, and believes
The house must have done something horrible
To the people who once lived here

Because now it is so desperately empty,
It must have done something to the sky
Because the sky, too, is utterly vacant
And devoid of meaning. There are no

Trees or shrubs anywhere—the house
Must have done something against the earth.
All that is present is a single pair of tracks
Straightening into the distance. No trains pass.

Now the stranger returns to this place daily
Until the house begins to suspect
That the man, too, is desolate, desolate
And even ashamed. Soon the house starts

To stare frankly at the man. And somehow
The empty white canvas slowly takes on
The expression of someone who is unnerved,
Someone holding his breath underwater.

And then one day the man simply disappears.
He is a last afternoon shadow moving
Across the tracks, making its way
Through the vast, darkening fields.

This man will paint other abandoned mansions,
And faded cafeteria windows, and poorly lettered
Storefronts on the edges of small towns.
Always they will have this same expression,

The utterly naked look of someone
Being stared at, someone American and gawky,
Someone who is about to be left alone
Again, and can no longer stand it.

Poor Angels

At this hour the soul floats weightlessly
through the city streets, speechless and invisible,
astonished by the smoky blend of grays and golds
seeping out of the air, the dark half-tones

of dusk already filling the cloudy sky
while the body sits listlessly by the window
sullen and heavy, too exhausted to move,
too weary to stand up or to lie down.

At this hour the soul is like a yellow wing
slipping through the treetops, a little ecstatic
cloud hovering over the sidewalks, calling out
to the approaching night, "Amaze me, amaze me,"

while the body sits glumly by the window
listening to the clear summons of the dead
transparent as glass, clairvoyant as crystal . . .
Some nights it is almost ready to join them.

Oh, this is a strained, unlikely tethering,
a furious grafting of the quick and the slow:
when the soul flies up, the body sinks down
and all night—locked in the same cramped room—

they go on quarreling, stubbornly threatening
to leave each other, wordlessly filling the air
with the sound of a low internal burning.
How long can this bewildering marriage last?

At midnight the soul dreams of a small fire
of stars flaming on the other side of the sky,
but the body stares into an empty night sheen,
a hollow-eyed darkness. Poor luckless angels,

feverish old loves: don't separate yet.
Let what rises live with what descends.

Wild Gratitude

Tonight when I knelt down next to our cat, Zooey,
And put my fingers into her clean cat's mouth,
And rubbed her swollen belly that will never know kittens,
And watched her wriggle onto her side, pawing the air,
And listened to her solemn little squeals of delight,
I was thinking about the poet, Christopher Smart,
Who wanted to kneel down and pray without ceasing
In every one of the splintered London streets,

And was locked away in the madhouse at St. Luke's
With his sad religious mania, and his wild gratitude,
And his grave prayers for the other lunatics,
And his great love for his speckled cat, Jeoffry.
All day today—August 13, 1983—I remembered how
Christopher Smart blessed this same day in August, 1759,
For its calm bravery and ordinary good conscience.

This was the day that he blessed the Postmaster General
"And all conveyancers of letters" for their warm humanity,
And the gardeners for their private benevolence
And intricate knowledge of the language of flowers,
And the milkmen for their universal human kindness.
This morning I understood that he loved to hear—
As I have heard—the soft clink of milk bottles
On the rickety stairs in the early morning,

And how terrible it must have seemed
When even this small pleasure was denied him.
But it wasn't until tonight when I knelt down
And slipped my hand into Zooey's waggling mouth
That I remembered how he'd called Jeoffry "the servant
Of the Living God duly and daily serving Him,"
And for the first time understood what it meant.
Because it wasn't until I saw my own cat
Whine and roll over on her fluffy back
That I realized how gratefully he had watched
Jeoffry fetch and carry his wooden cork
Across the grass in the wet garden, patiently
Jumping over a high stick, calmly sharpening
His claws on the woodpile, rubbing his nose
Against the nose of another cat, stretching, or
Slowly stalking his traditional enemy, the mouse,
A rodent, "a creature of great personal valour,"
And then dallying so much that his enemy escaped.

And only then did I understand
It is Jeoffry—and every creature like him—
Who can teach us how to praise—purring
In their own language,
Wreathing themselves in the living fire.

Indian Summer

It must have been a night like this one,
Cool and transparent and somehow even-tempered,
Sitting on the friendly wooden porch of someone's
Summer house in mid-October in the country

That my father, home from the Korean War
And still in uniform, wearing a pilot's bars
And carrying a pilot's stark memories (still
Fingering a parachute in the back of his mind)

Jumped from the front steps where he'd been sitting
And held a sweating gin and tonic in the air
Like a newly won trophy, and flushed and smiled
Into the eyes of a strangely willing camera.

It must have been winning to see him again
Safely home at the close of a vague war
That was too far away to imagine clearly,
A little guarded and shy, but keenly present,

Tall and solid and actual as ever, and anyway
Smiling past the camera at his high-school sweetheart
(Now his wife, mother of his two small children)
Surrounded by friends on a calm midwestern night.

It must have been so soothing to have him back
That no one studied him closely, no one noticed
That there was something askew, something
Dark and puzzling in his eyes, something deeply

Reluctant staring into the narrow, clear-eyed
Lens of the camera. I've imagined it all—
And tonight, so many light years afterwards,
Looking intently at a torn photograph

Of that young soldier, my distant first father,
Home from a war that he never once mentioned,
I can foresee the long winter of arguments
Ahead, the hard seasons of their divorce,

The furious battles in court, and beyond that,
The unexpected fire, the successive bankruptcies,
The flight to California with a crisp new bankroll,
The move to Arizona with a brand-new family.

Tonight the past seems as sharp and inevitable
As the moment in Indian Summer when you glance up
From a photograph album and discover the fireflies
Pulsing in the woods in front of the house

And the stars blackening in a thicket of clouds . . .
It must have been a night like this one
When my mother glanced over her husband's head
Into a cluster of trees emerging behind him

And heard the wind scraping against the branches
Like the *strop strop* of a razor on rawhide,
And saw the full moon rising between the clouds
And shattering into hundreds of glassy fragments.

The Skokie Theatre

Twelve years old and lovesick, bumbling
and terrified for the first time in my life,
but strangely hopeful, too, and stunned,
definitely stunned—I wanted to cry,
I almost started to sob when Chris Klein
actually touched me—oh God—below the belt
in the back row of the Skokie Theatre.
Our knees bumped helplessly, our mouths
were glued together like flypaper, our lips
were grinding in a hysterical grimace
while the most handsome man in the world
twitched his hips on the flickering screen
and the girls began to scream in the dark.
I didn't know one thing about the body yet,
about the deep foam filling my bones,
but I wanted to cry out in desolation
when she touched me again, when the lights
flooded on in the crowded theatre
and the other kids started to file
into the narrow aisles, into a lobby
of faded purple splendor, into the last
Saturday in August before she moved away.
I never wanted to move again, but suddenly
we were being lifted toward the sidewalk

in a crush of bodies, blinking, shy,
unprepared for the ringing familiar voices
and the harsh glare of sunlight, the brightness
of an afternoon that left us gripping
each other's hands, trembling and changed.

Commuters

It's that vague feeling of panic
That sweeps over you
Stepping out of the #7 train
At dusk, thinking, *This isn't me*
Crossing a platform with the other
Commuters in the worried half-light
Of evening, *that must be*

Someone else with a newspaper
Rolled tightly under his arm
Crossing the stiff, iron tracks
Behind the train, thinking, *This*
Can't be me stepping over the tracks
With the other commuters, slowly crossing
The parking lot at the deepest
Moment of the day, wishing

That I were someone else, wishing
I were anyone else but a man
Looking out at himself as if
From a great distance,
Turning the key in his car, starting
His car and swinging it out of the lot,

Watching himself grinding uphill
In a slow fog, climbing past the other
Cars parked on the side of the road,
The cars which seem ominously empty

And strange,
                and suddenly thinking
With a new wave of nausea
This isn't me sitting in this car
Feeling as if I were about to drown

In the blue air, *that must be*
Someone else driving home to his
Wife and children on an ordinary day
Which ends, like other days,
With a man buckled into a steel box,
Steering himself home and trying
Not to panic

In the last moments of nightfall
When the trees and the red-brick houses
Seem to float under green water
And the streets fill up with sea lights.

The Village Idiot

No one remembers him anymore, a boy
who carried his mattress through the town at dusk
searching for somewhere to sleep, a wild-eyed
relic of the Old World shrieking at a cow
in an open pasture, chattering with the sheep,
sitting alone on the front steps of the church,
gnawing gently at his wrist. He was tall
and ungainly, an awkward swimmer who could swim
the full length of the quarry in an afternoon,
swimming back on his back in the evening, though
he could also sit on the hillside for days
like a dim-witted pelican staring at the fish.
Now that he is little more than a vague memory,
a stock character in old stories, another bewildering
extravagance from the past—like a speckled seal
or an auk slaughtered off the North Atlantic rocks—
no one remembers the day that the village children
convinced him to climb down into an empty well
and then showered him for hours with rocks and mud,
or the night that a drunken soldier slit his tongue
into tiny shreds of cloth, darkened with blood.
He disappeared long ago, like the village itself,
but some mornings you can almost see him again
sleeping on a newspaper in the stairwell, rummaging
through a garbage can in the alley. And some nights
when you are restless and too nervous to sleep

you can almost catch a glimpse of him again
staring at you with glassy, uncomprehending eyes
from the ragged edges of an old photograph
of your grandfather, from the corner of a window
fogging up in the bathroom, from the wet mirror.

Three Journeys

Whoever has followed the bag lady
on her terrible journey past Food Lane's Super-Market,
and Maze's Records, and The Little Flowering Barbershop
on the southeast corner of Woodward and Euclid
will know what it meant for John Clare
to walk eighty miles across pocked and jutted
roads to Northborough, hungry, shy of strangers,
"foot foundered and broken down" after escaping
from the High Beech Asylum near Epping Forest.
And whoever has followed the bag lady
on her studious round of littered stairwells
and dead-end alleys, and watched her combing
the blue and white city garbage cans for empties,
and admired the way that she can always pick out
the single plate earring and one Canadian dime
from a million splinters of glass in a phone booth
will know how John Clare must have looked
as he tried to follow the route that a gypsy
had pointed out for him, scaling the high
palings that stood in his way, bruising
his feet on the small stones, stooping to
admire the pileworts and cowslips, scorning
the self-centered cuckoos but knowing the sweet
kinship of a landrail hiding in the hedgerows.

I began this morning by standing
in front of the New World Church's ruined storefront;
I was listening to the bag lady and a pimply-
faced old drunk trading secrets with the vent man,
and remembering how a gentleman on horseback
had mistaken John Clare for a broken-down haymaker
and tossed him a penny for a half-pint of beer.
I remembered how grateful he was to stand
elbow to elbow in the Old Plough Public House
happily sheltered from a sudden rainfall.
But later when I saw the bag lady
sprawled out on a steaming vent for warmth
I remembered how Clare had moved on, crippled
by tiny bits of gravel lodged in his shoes,
and how he tried to escape from the harsh wind
by lying down in an open dike bottom
but was soaked through clear to his bones;
how he came to the heavy wooden doors
of the Wild Ram Public House hours later,
and gazed longingly at the brightly lit windows,
and had no money, and passed on. Whoever
has stood alone in the night's deep shadows
listening to laughter coming from a well-lit house
will know that John Clare's loneliness was unbending.
And whoever has felt that same unbending loneliness
will also know what an old woman felt today
as she followed an obedient path between the huge
green garbage cans behind Kroger's Super-Market
and the small silver ones behind Clarence's grocery.

I began this day by following a bag lady
in honor of John Clare but suddenly, tonight,
I was reading "The Journey Out of Essex, 1841,"
in honor of the unknown bag lady.
I had witnessed a single day in her life
and was trying hard not to judge myself
and judging myself anyway.
I remember how she stooped to rub her foot;
how she smiled a small toothful grin
when she discovered a half-eaten apple;
how she talked on endlessly to herself
and fell asleep leaning against a broken wall
in an abandoned wooden shed on Second Avenue.
Tonight when I lie down in the dark
in my own bed, I want to remember
that John Clare was so desperately hungry
after three days and nights without food
that he finally knelt down, as if in prayer,
and ate the soft grass of the earth,
and thought it tasted like fresh bread,
and judged no one, not even himself,
and slept peacefully again, like a child.

In Spite of Everything, the Stars

Like a stunned piano, like a bucket
of fresh milk flung into the air
or a dozen fists of confetti
thrown hard at a bride
stepping down from the altar,
the stars surprise the sky.
Think of dazed stones
floating overhead, or an ocean
of starfish hung up to dry. Yes,
like a conductor's expectant arm
about to lift toward the chorus,
or a juggler's plates defying gravity,
or a hundred fastballs fired at once
and freezing in midair, the stars
startle the sky over the city.

And that's why drunks leaning up
against abandoned buildings, women
hurrying home on deserted side streets,
policemen turning blind corners, and
even thieves stepping from alleys
all stare up at once. Why else do
sleepwalkers move toward the windows,
or old men drag flimsy lawn chairs
onto fire escapes, or hardened criminals
press sad foreheads to steel bars?

Because the night is alive with lamps!
That's why in dark houses all over the city
dreams stir in the pillows, a million
plumes of breath rise into the sky.

Dawn Walk

Some nights when you're asleep
Deep under the covers, far away,
Slowly curling yourself back
Into a childhood no one
Living will ever remember
Now that your parents touch hands
Under the ground
As they always did upstairs
In the master bedroom, only more
Distant now, deaf to the nightmares,
The small cries that no longer
Startle you awake but still
Terrify me so that
I do get up, some nights, restless
And anxious to walk through
The first trembling blue light
Of dawn in a calm snowfall.
It's soothing to see the houses
Asleep in their own large bodies,
The dreamless fences, the courtyards
Unscarred by human footprints,
The huge clock folding its hands
In the forehead of the skyscraper
Looming downtown. In the park
The benches are layered in
White, the statue out of history
Is an outline of blue snow. Cars,
Too, are rimmed and motionless

Under a thin blanket smoothed down
By the smooth maternal palm
Of the wind. So thanks to the
Blue morning, to the blue spirit
Of winter, to the soothing blue gift
Of powdered snow! And soon
A few scattered lights come on
In the houses, a motor coughs
And starts up in the distance, smoke
Raises its arms over the chimneys.
Soon the trees suck in the darkness
And breathe out the light
While black drapes open in silence.
And as I turn home where
I know you are already awake,
Wandering slowly through the house
Searching for me, I can suddenly
Hear my own footsteps crunching
The simple astonishing news
That we are here,
Yes, we are still here.

From

The Night Parade

(1989)

Memorandums

"I feel anxious to insert these memorandums of my affections . . ."
—JOHN CLARE

I put down these memorandums of my affections
    To stave off the absolute,
  To stave off the flat palm of the wind
      Pressed against the forehead of night,
    To stave off the thought of stars
Swallowed by the constellations of darkness.

Winter descends in knives, in long sheets of ice
    Unravelling in the sky,
  In stuttering black syllables of rain.
      There's a vise grinding on my temples
  And the sound of a hammer thudding
Somewhere far back in my mind. I can't sleep,

And when I sleep I dream of murky chemicals
    Washing across the faces
  Of my grandparents floating face down
      In a swimming pool. I dream of un-
    Born children drifting overhead
And out of reach. I dream of blinding lights.

I put down these memorandums of my affections
    In honor of my mother
And my mother's mother who cooled
    My forehead with a damp washcloth,

My two sisters and the aunt
Who ministered to my headaches in childhood,

My grandfather who kissed me on the upper arm
        And tucked me in
    At night, my father who touched
        The blanket in the morning, gently.
        I think of my mother-in-law
And my friend—my only brother—who died

Because cancer feasted on their ripe bodies
        From the inside.
    I remember the ravaged stillness
        And peacefulness of their faces,
        Their open lips and sealed eyes
As they were zippered in bags and carted away.

I put down these memorandums of my affections
        In honor of tenderness,
    In honor of all those who have been
        Conscripted into the brotherhood
        Of loss, who have survived
The ice and the winter descending in knives.

We will be lifted up and carried a far distance
        On invisible wings
    And then set down in an empty field.
        We will carry our hearts in our bodies
        Over shadowy tunnels and bridges.
Someday we will let them go again, like kites.

My Grandmother's Bed

How she pulled it out of the wall
To my amazement. How it rattled and
Creaked, how it sagged in the middle
And smelled like a used-clothing store.
I was ecstatic to be sleeping on wheels!

It rolled when I moved; it trembled
When she climbed under the covers
In her flannel nightgown, kissing me
Softly on the head, turning her back.
Soon I could hear her snoring next to me—

Her clogged breath roaring in my ears,
Filling her tiny apartment like the ocean
Until I, too, finally swayed and slept
While a radiator hissed in the corner
And traffic droned on Lawrence Avenue . . .

I woke up to the color of light pouring
Through the windows, the odor of soup
Simmering in the kitchen, my grandmother's
Face. It felt good to be ashore again
After sleeping on rocky, unfamiliar waves.

I loved to help her straighten the sheets
And lift the Murphy back into the wall.
It was like putting the night away
When we closed the wooden doors again
And her bed disappeared without a trace.

My Grandfather's Poems

I remember that he wrote them backwards,
In Yiddish, in tiny, slanting, bird-like lines
That seemed to rise and climb off the page
In a flurry of winged letters, mysterious signs.

Scrupulously he copied them out
On the inside covers of his favorite books
While my sister and I romped through the house
Acting like cops and robbers, cowboys and crooks,

Whooping, shouting, and gunning each other down
In the hallway between rooms, mimicking fright,
Staggering from wall to bloody wall before
Collapsing in wild giggles at his feet.

Always he managed to quiet us again,
Kissing us each on the upper part of the arm,
Tucking us in . . . We never said prayers,
But later I could hear him in the next room

Talking to himself in a low, tearing whisper—
All I could fathom was a haunted sound
Like a rushing of waves in the distance,
Or the whoosh of treetops in the back yard.

For years I fell asleep to the rhythm
Of my grandfather's voice rising and falling,
Filling my head with his lost, unhappy poems:
Those faint wingbeats, that hushed singing.

Incandescence at Dusk

—Homage to Dionysius the Areopagite

There is fire in everything,
            shining and hidden—
Or so the saint believed. And I believe the saint:
Nothing stays the same
                in the shimmering heat
Of dusk during Indian summer in the country.

Out here it is possible to perceive
That those brilliant red welts
                    slashed into the horizon
Are like a drunken whip
                    whistling across a horse's back,
And that round ball flaring in the trees
Is like a coal sizzling
            in the mouth of a desert prophet.

Be careful.
Someone has called the orange leaves
                        sweeping off the branches
The colorful palmprints of God
                    brushing against our faces.
Someone has called the banked piles
                        of twigs and twisted veins
The handprints of the underworld
Gathering at our ankles and burning
                        through the soles of our feet.
We have to bear the sunset deep inside us.

I don't believe in ultimate things.
I don't believe in the inextinguishable light
                        of the other world.
I don't believe that we will be lifted up
                        and transfixed by radiance.
One incandescent dusky world is all there is.

But I like this vigilant saint
Who stood by the river at nightfall
And saw the angels descending
                        as burnished mirrors and fiery wheels,
As living creatures of fire,
                as streams of white flame . . .

1500 years in his wake,
I can almost imagine
                his disappointment and joy
When the first cool wind
                        starts to rise on the prairie,
When the soothing blue rain begins
                        to fall out of the cerulean night.

A Short Lexicon of Torture
in the Eighties

That's not a man in pain
                              but *a Brazilian phone*—
It won't be making any outgoing calls.

That's not a woman sprawling on the floor
But *an old-fashioned dance,*
                              like the tango.

Pull up a chair with a knotted rope.
Let's have *a tea party with toast*
                              and *hors d'oeuvres.*

Let's take a seat
                 on *the parrot's perch.*
Let's rock to *the motorola* with headphones.

Do you want to bathe
                     in the porcelain tub?
Do you want to sing to *the little hare?*

Let's stroll over to *the guest room.*
Let's take a bus ride
                     to *the San Juanica bridge.*

Forget the ovens and smokestacks.
Forge *the rack and screw,*
                     the tiger's cage.

We're celebrating *a birthday party*
                                    in your honor.
We're lighting candles on your favorite cake.

We're taking you to *a parade*
                                    on a sandy beach.
You're going down in *a submarine.*

Execution

The last time I saw my high school football coach
He had cancer stenciled into his face
Like pencil marks from the sun, like intricate
Drawings on the chalkboard, small *x*'s and *o*'s
That he copied down in a neat numerical hand
Before practice in the morning. By day's end
The board was a spiderweb of options and counters,
Blasts and sweeps, a constellation of players
Shining under his favorite word, *Execution,*
Underlined in the upper right-hand corner of things.
He believed in football like a new religion
And had perfect, unquestioning faith in the fundamentals
Of blocking and tackling, the idea of warfare
Without suffering or death, the concept of teammates
Moving in harmony like the planets—and yet
Our awkward adolescent bodies were always canceling
The flawless beauty of Saturday afternoons in September,
Falling away from the particular grace of autumn,
The clear weather, the ideal game he imagined.
And so he drove us through punishing drills
On weekday afternoons, and doubled our practice time,
And challenged us to hammer him with forearms,
And devised elaborate, last-second plays—a flea-
Flicker, a triple reverse—to save us from defeat.
Almost always they worked. He despised losing
And loved winning more than his own body, maybe even
More than himself. But the last time I saw him
He looked wobbly and stunned by illness,

And I remembered the game in my senior year
When we met a downstate team who loved hitting
More than we did, who battered us all afternoon
With a vengeance, who destroyed us with timing
And power, with deadly, impersonal authority,
Machine-like fury, perfect execution.

In the Underground Garage

I pulled my mother's baby-blue Thunderbird
Into a parking garage on the corner of Michigan and Lake
On a late afternoon in mid-December, one
Of those slushy Chicago dusks
When the air thickens around the Christmas lights
Strung through the evergreens that line the sidewalks,
And the diligent rush-hour traffic creeps along the lakeside
As if in obedience to a secret commandment,
And the shoppers sift through the fog.
The car hummed on the downward-spiraling ramp
And glided to a halt in front of a booth
Where a familiar-looking attendant in uniform—
I didn't recognize him at first—
Threw open a steel door and became
My closest friend from high school
Turning away in embarrassment. In a moment
We were in each other's arms,
But he wouldn't say a word
And already the cars were piling up behind us,
A row of impatience. He held the keys
To my mother's car and shifted his weight
Back on his heels—half in anger, half in disappointment—
As I saw him do on the sidelines against Maine South,
A linebacker's helmet imprinted on my back.
For an instant, I can see us
Putting our heads together in Jake's Diner
Over the memory of kisses from Marcia and Betty-Anne,
Or driving into Niles Township

For a beer-run in his father's pea-green Nova.
We were working side by side
In the old factory buried below Monroe Street,
Taking orders from the foreman on the second floor
And stacking cartons on top of cartons
On top of heavy wooden skids . . .
But he didn't want to remember the past
Before our futures divided, before
Whatever was going to happen between us
Had already happened. The honking began
In earnest and the cars formed
A snake-like line curving up to the street,
Like souls in purgatory.
I thought of his father's labor
On the corrugator and the printing press, the years
His mother worked the night shift at Billings Container.
But before I could ask about them,
My friend slammed the door and screeched away
In the glistening blue car of privilege.
In silence he left me
Staring after him through the fog
And steam rising from the grated vents
At the buttresses and concrete dividers,
The spaces misting between us, the cars
Rolling into the underground depths at nightfall,
Filled with ghosts and strangers.

The Abortion (1969)

I swore I'd always remember
That dingy hotel room in downtown Detroit
Where the doctor came
                with his gleaming metallic instruments
To carve a newly-forming body
                    out of your body
For 500 dollars in small bills paid in cash.

I swore I'd never forget the exact pressure
Of your hand in mine
             as he prodded open your legs
With a surgical knife
             under a tent of white sheets
While his girlfriend fiddled with the radio
And lounged against the door in her spiked heels.

Afterwards, I remembered three shades of blood
                      staining the bedsheets,
How the doctor sudsed his hands
               carefully in the sink,
Turning them over twice in the bathroom light.
I remembered the door shutting behind them,
The sound of heels clicking in the hallway
                 as an elevator rang in the distance
And I stared into your ashen face . . .

That night I believed your heavy narcotic sleep
Would never end,
                    I cradled your face in my palms
Like a fragile sculpture
And wiped your dampening forehead
                              with a cool washcloth.
It wasn't enough. Nothing helped but rest,
Your body already trying
                    to knit up the emptiness.

I can still feel the relief of that next morning
When you woke up with a surprised moan
                              and a pained smile on your face,
When I saw the fresh light
                    crystallizing on your body
As if an angel had sprung back to life.

It's touching to remember us
                    in the early morning light,
Two teenagers holding hands on a narrow bed,
A boy and a girl
                    not knowing what they've done,
Murderous children lying together in innocence,
An electric joy
          passing back and forth between them . . .

That was before we told your parents about it,
Before we discovered
                         you had never been pregnant,
Before the doctor was arrested
                                  in a dank hotel room
With a young assistant at his side.

That was before you turned to me years later
In the rain, in a different city,
Almost apologizing
After so much had gone wrong between us,
Saying,
          I'll never forgive you. Nothing is forgiven.

Infertility

We don't know how to name
                                    the long string of zeros
Stretching across winter,
                                    the barren places,
The missing birthdates of the unborn.

We'd like to believe in their souls
                                    drifting through space
Between the Crab and the Northern Cross,
Smoky and incandescent,
                                    longing for incarnation.

We'd like to believe in their spirits descending,
But month after month, year after year,
We have laid ourselves down
                                    and raised ourselves up
And not one has ever entered our bodies.

We'd like to believe that we have planted
And tended seeds
                    in their honor,
But the spirits never appear
                                    in darkness or light.

We don't know whether to believe in their non-existence
Or their secrecy and evasiveness,

                        their invisible spite.
Maybe it's past us, maybe it's the shape of nothing
Being born,

           the cold slopes of the absolute.

From

Earthly Measures

(1994)

Uncertainty

We couldn't tell if it was a fire in the hills
Or the hills themselves on fire, smoky yet
Incandescent, too far away to comprehend.
And all this time we were traveling toward
Something vaguely burning in the distance—
A shadow on the horizon, a fault line—
A blue and cloudy peak which never seemed
To recede or get closer as we approached.
And that was all we knew about it
As we stood by the window in a waning light
Or touched and moved away from each other
And turned back to our books. But it remained
Even so, like the thought of a coal fading
On the upper left-hand side of our chests,
A destination that we bore within ourselves.
And there were those—were they the lucky ones?—
Who were unaware of rushing toward it.
And the blaze awaited them, too,

Four A.M.

The hollow, unearthly hour of night.
Swaying vessel of emptiness.

Patron saint of dead planets
and vast, unruly spaces receding in mist.

Necklace of shattered constellations:
soon the stars will be extinguished.

A cellblock sealed in ice.
An icehouse sealed in smoke.

The hour when nothing begets nothing,
the hour of drains and furnaces,

shadows fastened to a blank screen
and the moon floating in a pool of ashes.

The hour of nausea at middle age,
the hour with its face in its hands,

the hour when no one wants to be awake,
the scorned hour, the very pit

of all the other hours,
the very dirge.

Let five o'clock come
with its bandages of light.

A life buoy in bruised waters.
The first broken plank of morning.

Man on a Fire Escape

He couldn't remember what propelled him
out of the bedroom window onto the fire escape
of his fifth-floor walkup on the river,

so that he could see, as if for the first time,
sunset settling down on the dazed cityscape
and tugboats pulling barges up the river.

There were barred windows glaring at him
from the other side of the street
while the sun deepened into a smoky flare

that scalded the clouds gold-vermilion.
It was just an ordinary autumn twilight—
the kind he had witnessed often before—

but then the day brightened almost unnaturally
into a rusting, burnished, purplish red haze
and everything burst into flame:

the factories pouring smoke into the sky,
the trees and shrubs, the shadows
of pedestrians singed and rushing home . . .

There were storefronts going blind and cars
burning on the parkway and steel girders
collapsing into the polluted waves.

Even the latticed fretwork of stairs
where he was standing, even the first stars
climbing out of their sunlit graves

were branded and lifted up, consumed by fire.
It was like watching the start of Armageddon,
like seeing his mother dipped in flame . . .

And then he closed his eyes and it was over.
Just like that. When he opened them again
the world had reassembled beyond harm.

So where had he crossed to? Nowhere.
And what had he seen? Nothing. No foghorns
called out to each other, as if in a dream,

and no moon rose over the dark river
like a warning—icy, long-forgotten—
while he turned back to an empty room.

Scorched

It comes back to me as the enigma
of doorways and clocktowers, of standing
by an open window drenched in sunlight

and staring down at a drowsy piazza
where a waiter eternally cleans a table
and two cats squirm in the shadows.

Three p.m.: the hour of scorched absences,
the hour when the city slumps like a widow
and a dogged couple in their thirties

is forever trying to wring a child
from the clamor of each other's bodies
in a small pensione of the old quarter.

Look at them breathing against each other
in the hour of silences, the hour
of nothing violated and nothing affirmed,

of pleasure mixed with the fire of grief.
It is the wounded rite of infertility,
the inconceivable zero in the heart

of summer, the cancellation, the void
where what cannot be born is not born
and what does not exist will never exist.

Look at them cooling in each other's arms:
two muffled bells molded from the heat,
two bodies cast from the bright flames.

In Memoriam Paul Celan

Lay these words into the dead man's grave
next to the almonds and black cherries—
tiny skulls and flowering blood-drops, eyes,
and Thou, O bitterness that pillows his head.

Lay these words on the dead man's eyelids
like eyebrights, like medieval trumpet flowers
that will flourish, this time, in the shade.
Let the beheaded tulips glisten with rain.

Lay these words on his drowned eyelids
like coins or stars, ancillary eyes.
Canopy the swollen sky with sunspots
while thunder addresses the ground.

Syllable by syllable, clawed and handled,
the words have united in grief.
It is the ghostly hour of lamentation,
the void's turn, mournful and absolute.

Lay these words on the dead man's lips
like burning tongs, a tongue of flame.
A scouring eagle wheels and shrieks.
Let God pray to us for this man.

Simone Weil:
The Year of Factory Work (1934-1935)

A glass of red wine trembles on the table,
Untouched, and lamplight falls across her shoulders.

She looks down at the cabbage on her plate,
She stares at the broken bread. Proposition:

The irreducible slavery of workers. "To work
In order to eat, to eat in order to work."

She thinks of the punchclock in her chest,
Of night deepening in the bindweed and crabgrass,

In the vapors and atoms, in the factory
Where a steel vise presses against her temples

Ten hours per day. She doesn't eat.
She doesn't sleep. She almost doesn't think

Now that she has brushed against the bruised
Arm of oblivion and tasted the blood, now

That the furnace has labelled her skin
And branded her forehead like a Roman slave's.

Surely God comes to the clumsy and inefficient,
To welders in dark spectacles, and unskilled

Workers who spend their allotment of days
Pulling red-hot metal bobbins from the flames.

Surely God appears to the shattered and anonymous,
To the humiliated and afflicted

Whose legs are married to perpetual motion
And whose hands are too small for their bodies.

Proposition: "Through work man turns himself
Into matter, as Christ does through the Eucharist.

Work is like a death. We have to pass
Through death. We have to be killed."

We have to wake in order to work, to labor
And count, to fail repeatedly, to submit

To the furious rhythm of machines, to suffer
The pandemonium and inhabit the repetitions,

To become the sacrificial beast: time entering
Into the body, the body entering into time.

She presses her forehead against the table:
To work in order to eat, to eat . . .

Outside, the moths are flaring into stars
And stars are strung like beads across the heavens.

Inside, a glass of red wine trembles
Next to the cold cabbage and broken bread.

Exhausted night, she is the brimming liquid
And untouched food. Come down to her.

Away from Dogma

I was prevented by a sort of shame from going
into churches . . . Nevertheless, I had three
contacts with Catholicism that really counted.
　　　　　　　　　　—SIMONE WEIL

1. In Portugal

One night in Portugal, alone in a forlorn
village at twilight, escaping her parents,
she saw a full moon baptized on the water
and the infallible heavens stained with clouds.

Vespers at eventide. A ragged procession
of fishermen's wives moving down to the sea,
carrying candles onto the boats, and singing
hymns of heartrending sadness. She thought:

this world is a smudged blue village
at sundown, the happenstance of stumbling
into the sixth canonical hour, discovering
the tawny sails of evening, the afflicted

religion of slaves. She thought: I am
one of those slaves, but I will not kneel
before Him, at least not now, not with
these tormented limbs that torment me still.

God is not manifest in this dusky light
and humiliated flesh: He is not among us.
But still the faith of the fishermen's wives
lifted her toward them, and she thought:

this life is a grave, mysterious moment
of hearing voices by the water and seeing
olive trees stretching out in the dirt,
of accepting the heavens cracked with rain.

2. In Assisi

To stand on the parcel of land where the saint
knelt down and married Lady Poverty, to walk
through the grasses of the Umbrian hills
where he scolded wolves and preached

to doves and jackdaws, where he chanted
canticles to the creatures who share our earth,
praising Brother Sun who rules the day,
Sister Moon who brightens the night.

Brother Fire sleeps in the arms of Sister Water.
Brother Wind kisses Sister Earth so tenderly.
To carry a picnic and eat whatever he ate—
bread and wine, the fare of tourists and saints.

She disliked the Miracles in the Gospels.
She never believed in the mystery of contact,
here below, between a human being and God.
She despised popular tales of apparitions.

But that afternoon in Assisi she wandered
through the abominable Santa Maria degli Angeli
and happened upon a little marvel of Romanesque
purity where St. Francis liked to pray.

She was there a short time when something absolute
and omnivorous, something she neither believed
nor disbelieved, something she understood—
but what was it?—forced her to her knees.

3. At Solesmes

From Palm Sunday to Easter Tuesday,
from Matins to Vespers and beyond, from
each earthly sound that hammered her skull
and entered her bloodstream, from the headaches

she sent into the universe and took back
into her flesh, from the suffering body
to the suffering mind, from the unholy breath
to the memories that never forgot her—

the factory whistle and the branding-iron
of the masters, the sixty-hour work week
and the machine that belched into her face,
the burns that blossomed on her arms—

from whatever weighs us down to whatever
lifts us up, from whatever mutilates us
to whatever spirits us away, from soul
descending to soul arising, moment by moment

she felt the body heaped up and abandoned
in the corner, the skin tasted and devoured;
she felt an invisible hand wavering
over the rags she was leaving behind.

Between the voices chanting and her own recitation,
between the heartbeats transfigured to prayer,
between the word *forsaken* and the word *joy,*
God came down and possessed her.

The Reader

It waited for him in the dusty treatises
On his father's bookshelf, in the back stacks
Of the local library, in the rare book room
And the manuscript collection on the fifth floor,
In the basement where they kept the well-thumbed
Periodicals and crumbling theology texts.
Unshelved and displaced, uncatalogued, overdue,
It waited in the background while he scanned
The entries and noted the citations, memorizing
The names of authors, writing down titles.
It shuddered when he read about the infinite
Starry spaces and the fast-moving river
Into which he would never step twice,
And it paused in the margins of the ancients,
In archaic Greek rituals and thunderous voices
Rising out of the whirlwind. He could not
Hear it breathing between the pages, belabored
In German, trilling in Spanish, stammering
Backward in Hebrew. He did not listen
To it crying out softly in the trees
Like a prophecy, though it waited for him
Nonetheless, a patient and faithful oblivion,
An emptiness, which he would not call God.

The Welcoming

After the long drought
                    and the barren silence,
After seven years of fertility doctors
And medicine men in clinics
                    dreaming of rain,
After the rainfall and the drugs
                    that never engendered a child—

What is for others nature
                    is for us culture:
Social workers and lawyers,
                    home studies and courtrooms,
Passports, interlocutory orders, a birth certificate
        that won't be delivered for a year,
                    a haze of injunctions, jurisdictions, handshakes,
Everyone standing around in dark suits
                    saying yes, we think so, yes . . .

It has been less than a month and already
I want to bring you
                    out of the darkness,
                    out of the deep pockets of silence . . .
While you were spending your fifth day
                    under bright lights in a new world,
We were traveling
                    from Rome to New Orleans,
Twenty-three hours of anguish and airplanes,
Instructions in two languages,

music from cream-colored headsets,
        jet lag instead of labor,

And on the other end a rainbow
                        of streamers in the French Quarter,
        a row of fraternity boys celebrating
                in Jackson Square, the trolleys
                buzzing up and down St. Charles Avenue,
The stately run-down southern mansions
Winking
        behind the pecan trees and the dark-leaved magnolias.

You were out there somewhere,
                blinking, feeding omnivorously
                from a nurse's arms, sleeping,
But who could sleep anymore
                beside the innocent and the oblivious,
        who could dream?

How unreal it was to drive
                through the narrow, twisted streets
        of an unfamiliar American city
        and then arrive at the empty bungalow
                        of a friend of a friend.
Outside, the trees waved slightly
                        under a cradle of moonlight
While, inside, the floorboards sagged
                and creaked, the air conditioner kicked on
                        in the next room, in autumn,
        an invisible cat cried—a baby's cry—
        and roamed through the basement at 4 a.m.

All night long we were moored
               to the shoreline of the bay windows,
                              to the edge of a bent sky
               where the moon rocked
and the stars were tiny crescent fish
               swimming through amniotic fluids.
There was a deep rumbling underground,
And our feelings came in and went out, like waves.

By the vague tremors of dawn,
By the first faint pinkish-blue light
               of morning rising in the east,
All we could think about
               was the signing of papers
                              in a neighboring parish,
               the black phone that was going to shout
                              at any moment, just once,
       our lawyer's slow drive to the hospital
               with an infant seat
       strapped into her car. You were waiting:
Little swimmer, the nurses at Touro
               didn't want to relinquish you
                      to the afterlife of our arms . . .

But so it was written:

On the sixth day,
After five days and nights on this earth,
You were finally delivered
                      into our keeping,

A wrinkled traveler from a faraway place
                   who had journeyed a great distance,
A sweet aboriginal angel
                   with your own life,
A throbbing bundle of instincts and nerves—
          perfect fingers, perfect toes,
               shiny skin, blue soulful eyes
                    deeply set in your perfectly shaped head—

Oh wailing messenger,
Oh baleful full-bodied crier
                    of the abandoned and the chosen,
Oh trumpet of laughter, oh Gabriel,
                    joy everlasting . . .

Summer Surprised Us

These first days of summer are like the pail
of blueberries that we poured out together
into the iron sink in the basement—

a brightness unleashed and spilling over
with tiny bell-shaped flowers, the windows
opened and the shrubs overwhelming the house

like the memory of a forgotten country, Nature,
with its wandering migrations and changing borders,
its thickets, woodlands, bee-humming meadows . . .

These widening turquoise days in mid-June
remind me of slow drives through the country
with my parents, the roads spreading out

before us like the inexhaustible hours
of childhood itself, like the wildflowers
and fruit stands blooming along the highway,

the heat tingling on my skin that would
burn with the banked fires of adolescence
and the no less poignant ache of adulthood

on those long detours through the park
during the last rain-soaked nights of spring
and the first beach days of the season . . .

It's the leisurely amplitude of feeling
that rises out of these expanding afternoons,
the days facing outward, the city taking notice

of itself after all these months, off-duty,
wearing short sleeve shirts and sleeveless dresses
the color of sunlight, the texture of morning.

It's the way we move toward each other
at night, tired, giddy after a day together
or a day apart, flush with newborn plans

for a holiday from daily life, in reality.
We are festive and free-floating. We are
poured out like a bucket of wild berries.

Solstice

Remember how the city looked from the harbor
    in early evening: its brutal gaze
averted, its poised and certain countenance
    wavering with lights?

Remember how we sat in swaybacked chairs
    and marvelled at the brush fires
of dusk clear in the distance, the flames
    scrawled across the skyline

like a signature while currents shifted
    inside us? Ecstasy of fire-
works rising in midsummer, of fulvous sails
    flashing in the heat

and orange life buoys bobbing on the water;
    ecstasy of flares and secrets
and two bodies held aloft by desire . . .
    Judge us as you will,

but remember that we, too, lived once
    in the fullness of a moment
before the darkness took its turn with us
    and the night clamped shut.

Posthumous Orpheus

He wandered through a patchwork of open fields
And abandoned farmhouses, singing, but the rocks
Wouldn't budge and the trees refused to bend,
Rooted deeply in the ground, stolid, ungiving.
He sang with a grief that would have moved the land
If the land were listening to anything but its own
Hard processes, and he mourned with a music
That would have lifted the hearts of animals
Grazing in the pastures, except there were no
Animals to be seen anywhere, just a few scrawny
Crows scrounging for food. He sang of lost
Unstoried realms, of vows eternally broken,
His bride turning to shadows in the underworld
Because of him, but he never understood
That his voice was drowned out by the wind
Blowing incessantly across the Great Plains,
And by the steady hum of telephone wires
Stretching into nowhere, and by the whoosh
Of stray trucks whizzing by on the highway.
Eurydice was gone and there were no Maenads
To envy or ambush him, no one even to send
His head floating down the stream with a lyre.
The riverbeds were as dry as the brown wheatfields
And he was an alien among the pre-fab silos
And barbed-wire fences, the burnt grasses
Moving ceaselessly in place. No, for him
There was only the silence of a vacant sky
Deepening overhead, the glassy-eyed desolation

Of a flat, unforgiving landscape rolling on endlessly,
And the loneliness of a few scattered houses
Buried on the prairie. His seven priestly notes
Were lost in miles and miles of empty space,
And he mourned until he could mourn no longer—
A ghost of himself, of his own unheeded grief—
And then he gave up, defeated, and stopped singing.

Art Pepper

It's the broken phrases, the fury inside him.
Squiggling alto saxophone playing out rickets
And jaundice, a mother who tried to kill him
In her womb with a coat hanger, a faltering
God-like father. The past is a bruised cloud
Floating over the houses like a prophecy,
The terrible foghorns off the shore at San Pedro.

Lightning without thunder. Years without playing.
Years of blowing out smoke and inhaling fire,
Junk and cold turkey, smacking up, the habit
Of cooking powder in spoons, the eyedroppers,
The spikes. Tracks on both arms. Tattoos.
The hospital cells at Fort Worth, the wire cages
In the L. A. County, the hole at San Quentin.

And always the blunt instrument of sex, the pain
Bubbling up inside him like a wound, the small
Deaths. The wind piercing the sheer skin
Of a dark lake at dawn. The streets at 5 a.m.
After a cool rain. The smoky blue clubs.
The chords of Parker, of Young, of Coltrane.
Playing solo means going on alone, improvising,

Hitting the notes, ringing the changes.
It's clipped phrasing and dry ice in summer,
Straining against the rhythm, speeding it up,
Loping forward and looping back, finding the curl

In the wave, the mood in the air. It's
Splintered tones and furious double timing.
It's leaving the other instruments on stage

And blowing freedom into the night, into the faces
Of emptiness that peer along the bar, ghosts,
Shallow hulls of nothingness. Hatred of God.
Hatred of white skin that never turns black.
Hatred of Patti, of Dianne, of Christine.
A daughter who grew up without him, a stranger.
Years of being strung out, years without speaking.

Pauses and intervals, silence. A fog rolling
Across the ocean, foghorns in the distance.
A lighthouse rising from the underworld.
A moon swelling in the clouds, an informer,
A twisted white mouth of light. Scars carved
And crisscrossed on his chest. The memory
Of nodding out, the dazed drop-off into sleep.

And then the curious joy of surviving, joy
Of waking up in a dusky room to a gush
Of fresh notes, a tremoring sheet of sound.
Jamming again. Careening through the scales
For the creatures who haunt the night.
Bopping through the streets in a half-light
With Laurie on his arm, a witness, a believer.

The night is going to burst inside him.
The wind is going to break loose forever
From his lungs. It's the fury of improvising,
Of going on alone. It's the fierce clarity
Of each note coming to an end, distinct,
Glistening. The alto's full-bodied laughter.
The white grief-stricken wail.

Mergers and Acquisitions

Beyond junk bonds and oil spills,
beyond the collapse of Savings and Loans,
beyond liquidations and options on futures,
beyond basket trading and expanding foreign markets,
the Dow Jones industrial average, the Standard
& Poor's stock index, mutual funds, commodities,
beyond the rising tide of debits and credits,
opinion polls, falling currencies, the signs
for L. A. Gear and Coca Cola Classic,
the signs for U.S. Steel and General Motors,
hi-grade copper, municipal bonds, domestic sugar,
beyond fax it and collateral buildups,
beyond mergers and acquisitions, leveraged buyouts,
hostile takeovers, beyond the official policy
on inflation and the consensus on happiness,
beyond the national trends in buying and selling,
getting and spending, the market stalled
and the cost passed on to consumers,
beyond the statistical charts on prices,
there is something else that drives us, some
rage or hunger, some absence smoldering
like a childhood fever vaguely remembered
or half-perceived, some unprotected desire,
greed that is both wound and knife,
a failed grief, a lost radiance.

Earthly Light

—Homage to the Seventeenth-Century Dutch Painters

1

I thought of northern skies flooded
with blue and gray, of monochromatic clouds
and rain-soaked wind blowing across the plains.

I thought of a cold day in March flattened
like unbleached canvas and steeped
in vertiginous greens, of industrious

local gods who furnished the low provinces
with rivers and lakes, waterlogged forests
and icy streams racing toward the ocean.

Or maybe there is only one God who supplies
the world with shorelines and sand dunes,
sunstruck mornings and thunderous nights,

maybe there is one God who keeps dividing
the world into water and land. I wonder
if the Dutch artists who could liquefy

sunlight and crystallize air worshipped Him
when they painted the large, whitewashed
interiors of churches; I wonder

if they were stealing supernatural light
or giving back to Him an earthly one
when they purified the sunshine skimming

grasslands and illuminating rooftops, burnishing
windows and mirrors, falling across floors.
If painting is to be a form of prayer

(prayer which Weil called "unmixed attention"
and George Herbert "something understood,"
one form among a myriad of forms),

then the Dutch artists prayed obliquely
by turning away from the other world
and detailing the plenitude of this —

the aurora seeping in from the sea
each day, the light dispersed equally
(was this the first time in history?)

on stout-hearted peasants and wealthy
burghers in irreproachable frock coats,
on civic guards and lacemakers, regents

and *regentin,* blacksmiths, cobblers . . .
Such a well-lighted lucky moment—
as if God had cracked the wooden shutters

of daybreak and started the scurrying
commercial hours that grew into weeks
and months, grew into the years.

2

"This brave nation lives with all it possesses
on a volcano," Benjamin Constant wrote,
"the lava of which is water," wherefore

everything had to be fastened down
and displayed before it floated away,
everything had to be acquired and caught

by those careful virtuosos of daily life
who belonged to the Guild of St. Luke
and painted flowers in terra cotta vases

and bowls of overripe fruit, who coveted
immaculate surfaces and imitated
the sheen on an iced pewter pitcher,

the sudden glow of a kerosene lamp,
a goblet half-filled with burgundy,
pages in a crumbling book of maps.

They were derided as "drudging mimics"
and "little deceivers," as "common
footsoldiers in the army of art,"

but they never ceased preserving and
rearranging a world of fish markets,
drapers' shops, brothels, dance halls.

The summer days swelled like good fortune
and they walked on well-scoured sidewalks
and stared admiringly at gabled roofs

and touched brick walls baking in the sun.
They were artisans who spent entire days
tracing the radiant afternoon light,

outlining the daily pleasures and sufferings
of usual people, the Saturday nights
and Sunday mornings of human life—

a wedding feast, a village kermis.
Naturally God was invoked and addressed
in sermons calling for gratitude and charity;

naturally He was remembered and then ignored
while the days slowly began to fade,
the taverns filled with revellers,

and the painters continued to record
a new country's ruddy complexion
and only slightly surprised expression,

its slashed sleeves and plumed hats,
its prosperous, secure, vanishing
bourgeois moment in the sun.

The market and tavern scenes survive,
conversation pieces, kitchen sagas,
a drawing room holding its breath

on a Sunday afternoon in late October;
what has lasted are sumptuous tapestries
and silks that you can *see* rustling,

spiral staircases and Persian carpets,
the texture of the world reduced and glittering
on fresh maps hanging in the background.

There's a woman playing the theorbo
for two suitors, a girl in white
sitting confidently at the virginal,

a family making music for themselves
while the light slants through the window
and trees begin to tremble in the cold.

Because there's also a goldfinch chained
to its perch, a pregnant woman standing
in the window frame tearing up a letter,

an old man grinding pigments. The colors glow.
And who remembers the inhabitants
of the leper colony and the poorhouse?

Who remembers the cost of too much work
in cold studios, mounting debts
and miserly commissions, paintings

traded for clothes and groceries, drawings
bartered for drinks at the nearest tavern?
Who remembers the untalented apprentices?

What has survived are the household bonds,
flowers, oysters, lemons, flies,
scrupulous renderings of credible life.

And who else painted for posterity
such profiles of human comfort and wealth:
all those pearl earrings and lace collars,

the horn of plenty blowing in autumn
for the ships gliding into safe harbor
with spices and perfumes from the East?

Travelers are marvelling at the paintings
displayed in every stall at the fair,
but look at that self portrait of the artist:

what a terrible old man! Lines
have been chiselled into his face
and his eyes are burning.

I remember the warm day in winter
when I stood on a hotel balcony listening
to bells ringing in the distance.

I had just seen all those galleries
of seventeenth-century light slipping
through interior courtyards and alleys,

branding doors and ceilings, pressing down
lightly on the skulls of buildings.
I had just seen rhetorics of light flashing

on curtains and tablecloths, mirrors
and windows, old maps and well-preserved
canvases varnished and framed.

I was alone, and for a while I stared
into a sky washed clean by rain,
an atmosphere luminous and polished,

ready to ascend, transparent as wings.
I saw tugboats pulling heavy barges
up and down the ice-filled river

while a white disc flamed overhead
and bands of purple light that resembled
bruises drifted and gradually dispersed.

I thought of northern skies flooded
with blue and gray, of monochromatic clouds
and rain-soaked wind blowing across the plains.

I thought of a landscape flattened
like unbleached canvas and steeped
in vertiginous greens, of the artists

who could liquefy thickest sunlight,
and the tangible, earth-colored country
that was all there would be to paint.

That February day I looked directly
into a wintry, invisible world
and that was when I turned away

from the God or gods I had wanted
so long and so much to believe in.
That was when I hurried down the stairs

into a street already crowded with people.
Because this world, too, needs our unmixed
attention, because it is not heaven

but earth that needs us, because
it is only earth—limited, sensuous
earth that is so fleeting, so real.

From

On Love

(1998)

The Poet at Seven

He could be any seven-year-old on the lawn,
holding a baseball in his hand, ready to throw.
He has the middle-class innocence of an American,

except for his blunt features and dark skin
that mark him as a Palestinian or a Jew,
his forehead furrowed like a question,

his concentration camp eyes, nervous, grim,
and too intense. He has the typical
blood of the exile, the refugee, the victim.

Look at him looking at the catcher for a sign—
so violent and competitive, so unexceptional,
except for an ancestral lamentation,

a shadowy, grief-stricken need for freedom
laboring to express itself through him.

Ocean of Grass

The ground was holy, but the wind was harsh
and unbroken prairie stretched for hundreds of miles
so that all she could see was an ocean of grass.

Some days she got so lonely she went outside
and nestled among the sheep, for company.
The ground was holy, but the wind was harsh

and prairie fires swept across the plains,
lighting up the country like a vast tinderbox
until all she could see was an ocean of flames.

She went three years without viewing a tree.
When her husband finally took her on a timber run
she called the ground holy and the wind harsh

and got down on her knees and wept inconsolably,
and lived in a sod hut for thirty more years
until the world dissolved in an ocean of grass.

Think of her sometimes when you pace the earth,
our mother, where she was laid to rest.
The ground was holy, but the wind was harsh
for those who drowned in an ocean of grass.

American Summer

Each day was a time clock that scarcely moved,
a slow fist punching us in, punching us out,
electric heat smoldering in the purple air,

but each night was a towering white fly ball
to center field—"a can of corn"—coming down
through stars glittering above the diamond.

Each day was a pair of heavy canvas gloves
hoisting garbage cans into an omnivorous mouth
that crept through thoroughfares and alleys,

but each night was the feeling of a bat
coming alive in your hands, it was lining
the first good pitch for a sharp single.

That summer I learned to steal second base
by getting the jump on right-handed pitchers
and then sliding head-first into the bag.

I learned to drive my father's stick shift
and to park with my girlfriend at the beach,
our headlights beaming and running low.

I was a sixteen-year-old in the suburbs
and each day was another lesson in working,
a class in becoming invisible to others,

but each night was a Walt Whitman of holidays,
the clarity of a whistle at five p.m.,
the freedom of walking out into the open air.

Hotel Window

Aura of absence, vertigo of non-being—
could I ever express what happened?
It was nothing, really, or next to nothing.

I was standing at the window at dusk
watching the cabs or the ghosts of cabs
lining up on the other side of the street

like yellow ferryboats waiting to cross
a great divide. All afternoon the doorman
whistled through the shadows, Charon

slamming doors and shouting orders
at traffic piling up along the curb.
People got into cars and disappeared—

ordinary people, tourists, businessmen—
while fog thickened the city's features
and emptied out the color. I don't know

how long I stood there as darkness
inhabited air itself, but suddenly,
when it happened, everything seemed dis-

jointed, charged with non-existence,
as if a vast, drowned lake was rising
invisibly—permanently—from the ground.

At the same time nothing really changed,
footsteps still echoed in the hallway
and laughter flared up the stairwell,

the passengers flinging themselves into cabs
never noticed they were setting forth
on a voyage away from their bodies.

I felt within a sickening emptiness—
intangible, unruly—and I remember
lying down on the floor of the room . . .

Then the phone rang and it was over.
Nothing happened—it took only a moment—
and it was dizzying, relentless, eternal.

Idea of the Holy

Out of the doleful city of Dis
rising between the rivers

Out of the God-shaped hole in my chest
and the sacred groves of your body

Out of stars drilled through empty spaces
and Stones in My Passway at four a.m.

All those hours studying under the lamp
the First Cause and the Unmoved Mover

the circle whose circumference is
everywhere and whose center is nowhere

the Lord strolled under the oak tree at Mamre
at the hottest moment of the day

the Lord vacated a region within himself
and recoiled from the broken vessels

a God uncreated or else a God withdrawn
a God comprehended is no God

Out of subway stations and towering bridges
Out of murky waters and the wound of chaos

Out of useless walks under fire escapes
Be friends to your burning

I saw the sun convulsed in clouds
and the moon candescent in a ring of flame

souls I saw weeping on streetcorners
in a strangeness I could not name

O falling numinous world at dusk
O stunned and afflicted emptiness

After three days and nights without sleep
I felt something shatter within me

then I lay down on my cot motionless
and sailed to the far side of nothing

Two (Scholarly) Love Poems

1. Dead Sea Scrolls

I was like the words
    on a papyrus apocryphon
        buried in a cave at Qumran,

and you were the scholar
    I had been waiting for
        all my life, the one reader

who unravelled the scrolls
    and understood the language
        and deciphered its mysteries.

2. A Treatise on Ecstasy

Touching your body
    I was like a rabbi pouring
        over a treatise on ecstasy,
            the message hidden in the scrolls.

I remember our delirium
    as my fingers moved backwards
        across the page, letter by letter,
            word by word, sentence by sentence.

I was a devoted scholar
    patiently tracing the secret
        passages of a mysterious text.
            Our room became a holy place

  as my hands trembled
    and my voice shook
        when I recited the blessings
            of a book that burst into flames.

From *The Lectures on Love*

Denis Diderot

The strange, enlightening subject of love
creates its own universe of discourse,
which is the least susceptible to reason.
My colleague d'Alembert dreams always
of mathematical formulas, finding ways
to treat subjects with absolute reason
in a precise hierarchy of discourse,
and yet he is unprepared for love—

a subject which seems highly illogical.
One might even say that to embrace Eros
is to enter into a state of visionary
impetuousness with another human being.
D'Alembert suspects that I am being
petulant in my idea of the visionary
dimensions of what we think of as Eros;
he is skeptical of anything illogical

or involuntary, anything beyond reason,
and there is nothing beyond or past love
for no one in the world can explain why
it comes and goes of its own free will.
Eros is not subject to Rational Will
and it pains me that nobody knows why

the crooked course of people in love
can be acutely cruel beyond all reason.

Adam and Eve at the sacred beginning
stand as the first principle of love:
I have dreamt of Eros between equals—
warm-hearted, affectionate, appreciative
(I love you, and therefore I appreciate
our companionship as natural equals).
This serves as an introduction to love,
but only an entry, only a beginning;

for no greater wonder exists than love,
a brutal and creative human discovery.
I conceive desire—sexual love—as Eros,
and passion as the knowledge we embody:
an activity of mind as well as body.
For all those who have experienced Eros,
may these revelations help you discover
yourself the encyclopedia of love.

Giacomo Leopardi
Poetry Would Be a Way of Praising God
If God Existed

Deep in the heart of night
I stood on a hill in wintertime
and stared up at the baleful moon.
I was terrified of finding myself
in the midst of nothing, myself
nothingness clarified, like the moon.
I was suffocating inside time,
contemplating the empty night

when a bell rang in the distance
three times, like a heart beating
in the farthest reaches of the sky.
The music was saturated with stillness.
I stood listening to that stillness
until it seemed to fill the sky.
The moon was like a heart beating
somewhere far off in the distance.

But there is no heart in a universe
of dying planets, infinite starry spaces.
Death alone is the true mother of Eros
and only love can revivify the earth,
for what is this emptiness, the earth,
but a black sea pulsing without Eros
under infinitely dead starry spaces?
Love alone can redeem our universe.

Heinrich Heine

I come to you as a whole-hearted man.
I have had myself carried here today
on what we may call my mattress-grave
where I have been entombed for years
(forgive me if I don't stand up this time)
to speculate about the nature of love.

As a cripple talking about physical love,
a subject I've been giving up for years,
I know that my situation (this time
he's gone too far!) is comical and grave.
But don't I still appear to be a man?
Hath not a Jew eyes, etc., at least today?

I am an addict of the human comedy
and I admit every pleasure, especially love,
is like the marriage of the French and Germans
or the eternal quarrel between Space and Time.
We are all creeping madly toward the grave
or leaping forward across the years

(Me, I haven't been able to leap in years)
and bowing under the fiendish blows of Time.
All that can distract us—gentlemen, ladies—
is the splendid warfare between men and women.
I don't hesitate to call the struggle "love."
Look at me: my feverish body is a grave,

I've been living so long on a mattress-grave
that I scarcely even resemble a man,
but what keeps me going is the quest for love.
I may be a dog who has had his day
(admittedly a day that has lasted for years)
but I'm also a formidable intellect of our time

and I'm telling you nothing can redeem Time
or the evident oblivions of the grave
or the crippling paralysis of the years
except the usual enchantments of love.
That's why the night hungers for the day
and the gods—heaven help us—envy the human.

For man and woman, the days pass into years
and the body is a grave filled with time.
We are drowning. All that rescues us is love.

Charles Baudelaire

These speculations afford me great pleasure
beyond human hypocrisy. My subject is love
and my proposition a simple one: erotic love,
which is, after all, a fatal form of pleasure,
resembles a surgical operation, or torture.
Forgive me if I sound ironic or cynical
but, I'm certain you'll agree, cynicism
is sometimes needed in discussing torture.

Act One, Scene One: The score is "Love."
The setting of a great operatic passion.
At first the lovers have equal passion
but, it turns out, one always seems to love
the other less. He, or she, is the surgeon
applying a scalpel to the patient, the victim.
I know because I have been that victim;
I have also been the torturer, the surgeon.

Can you hear those loud spasmodic sighs?
Who hasn't uttered them in hours of love?
Who hasn't drawn them from his (or her) lover?
It's sacrilegious to call such noises "ecstasies"
when they're a species of decomposition,
surrendering to death. We can get drunk
on each other, but don't pretend being drunk
puts us in a sudden death-defying position.

Why are people so proud of that spellbound
look, that hard stiffening between the legs?
Example One: She ran her hand down my legs
until I felt I'd been gagged and bound.
Example Two: She no longer gave me pleasure,
nonetheless, I rested my hand on her nude body
casually, I leaned over and tasted her body
until her whole being trembled with pleasure.

The erotic is an intimate form of cruelty
and every pleasure can be used to prostitute
another: I love you and become your prostitute
but my generosity is your voluptuous cruelty.
Sex is humiliation, a terrifying game
in which one partner loses self-control.
The subject concerns ownership or control
and that makes it an irresistible game.

I once heard the question discussed:
Wherein consists love's greatest pleasure?
I pondered the topic with great pleasure
but the whole debate filled me with disgust.
Someone declared, *We love a higher power.*
Someone said, *Giving is better than receiving,*
though someone else retorted, *I prefer receiving.*
No one there ever connected love to power.

Someone truly announced, *The greatest pleasure*
in love is to populate the State with children.
But must we really be no better than children
whenever we discuss the topic of pleasure?
Pain, I say, is inseparable from pleasure
and love is but an exquisite form of torture.
You need me, but I carry the torch for her . . .
Evil comes enswathed in every pleasure.

Margaret Fuller

Thank you for attending this conversation on love.
I am going to argue in the Nineteenth Century
a woman can no longer be sacrificed for love.
The Middle Ages are over, ladies and gentlemen,

and I am going to argue in the Nineteenth Century
we are not merely wives, whores, and mothers.
The Middle Ages are over, ladies. And gentlemen,
we can now be sea captains, if you will.

We are not merely wives, whores, and mothers.
We can be lawyers, doctors, journalists,
we can now be sea captains, if you will.
What matters to us is our own fulfillment.

We can be lawyers, doctors, journalists
who write ourselves into the official scripts.
What matters to us is our own fulfillment.
It is time for Eurydice to call for Orpheus

and to sing herself into the official scripts.
She is no longer a stranger to her inheritance.
It is time for Eurydice to call for Orpheus
and to move the earth with her triumphant song.

She is no longer a stranger to her inheritance.
She, too, feels divinity within her body
and moves the earth with her triumphant song.
God created us for the purpose of happiness.

She, too, feels divinity within her body.
Our holiest work is to transform the earth.
God created us for the purpose of happiness.
The earth itself becomes a parcel of heaven.

Our holiest work is to transform the earth.
Thank you for attending this conversation on love.
The earth itself becomes a parcel of heaven.
A woman can no longer be sacrificed for love.

Tristan Tzara

There is no such thing as a dada lecture
a manifesto is addressed to the whole world
I am opposed to every system except one
love is irrational and you are the reason

a manifesto is addressed to the whole world
but bells ring out for no reason at all
love is irrational and you are the reason
I am a bridge harboring your darkness

but bells ring out for no reason at all
you are a fresh wind assaulted by sails
I am a bridge harboring your darkness
let's not lash ourselves to the flagpoles

you are a fresh wind assaulted by sails
I am a wound that sprays your salt
let's not lash ourselves to the flagpoles
let's not swim to the music of sailors

I am a wound that sprays your salt
ambassadors of sentiment hate our chorus
let's not swim to the music of sailors
we cast our anchors into the distance

ambassadors of sentiment hate our chorus
they can't pollute our smokiest feelings
we cast our anchors into the distance
we sail our boats for the netherworld

they can't pollute our smokiest feelings
each of us has a thousand virginities
we sail our boats for the netherworld
I'm giving you all my nothingness

each of us has a thousand virginities
we still consider ourselves charming
I'm giving you all my nothingness
I have doubted everything but this

we still consider ourselves charming
there is no such thing as a dada lecture
I have doubted everything but this
I am opposed to every system except one

Gertrude Stein

Love happens to be an astonishing state,
a state in which all of us are astonished.

Everyone asks questions of this state
and then the state asks questions of everyone.

It's a country with a queer feeling
for the state, no apologies are necessary.

I should not neglect hapless exchanges:
what does she mean by laughing at me?

I should not neglect secrets and dungeons,
mistakes, confessions in tears at midnight.

Anger is pungent, but forgiveness is sweet.
I never knew this fruit until I tasted it.

It's infamous. We never trusted the garden
until we were expelled from it, together.

The pink melon has the flavor of joy,
but you must peel it, deliciously.

I like to be seized here and here.
Touch me again, my spoiled pugilist.

I was aghast at your red houseslippers,
but I admit to adoring your feet.

Don't deny it. For a time we were plagued
by baby-talk, toothlessness, bonbons.

We recovered nicely, my dark magic.
You are a hat pulled out of my rabbit.

Did I mention gaiety, fancy summer balls,
your blue dress with exquisite buttons?

I like it when we eat on moving trains.
The food slides a little under our manners.

We came home and cleaned the closets.
Look at these natty stockings. Rip!

We laughed until our sides split.
We split until our sides laughed.

Once, we were so annoyed by newspapers
we blamed each other for being sick.

The slamming door can be lonesome.
Some aloneness. The door slamming.

Adverse to verse, I added verses,
stanzas against her shackles. Versus.

She pruned my puns. I smoked and fumed.
How lousy to be jealous. The sweet louse.

Since when do plants know our names:
love-in-a-mist, love-lies-bleeding.

It's dangerous out there in the tropics.
Would you like some tea? Kisses. More.

A lice had lice, and the lice had Alice.
The parlor was atrocious. How lascivious.

So I am splashed again by paintings:
your colorful looks make me giddy.

We are pleased by our great fortune.
In the midst of our fortune we are pleased.

You are my passport to a lovely estate.
I have something stately to declare.

Not surprising I like to make sentences.
The sentences themselves are surprised.

I'd like to know if happiness is
a sentence, a question, or an exclamation.

All of us are astonished by love.
Love happens to be. An astonishing state.

Marina Tsvetaeva

Human thresholds are meant to be crossed,
so please come in and make yourself at home.
I'm certainly not going to deliver *A Lecture
on Love* (what an insufferable word, "lecture"),
though I shall speak about the essential home-
lessness of love, always star-crossed . . .

I have a talent for "non-reciprocal love"
and all my work is an argument for rapture.
When you love a person you always want him
to disappear so your mind can work on him.
The imagination is a storm-cloud of rapture
which I have scattered, like unhappy love.

"A person has to be condemned to poetry
like a wolf to his howling," A. Bely said,
"but you're a bird that keeps on singing."
I like to be torn apart by my own singing,
like one of Odysseus's men who, it's said,
destroyed himself for the Siren's poetry.

"I have lived with the shudder of longing"
(M. V. wrote), insatiable for the genuine.
I have held a boiling teapot, a frying pan,
a broom, an iron, three babies, and a pen
that stutters with knowledge of the genuine:
I have been hollowed out by sexual longing,

and I've paid for my transcendental passion.
What poet actually *isn't* a Negro, a woman,
or a Jew who has been slain by gentiles?
I know because I've lived among gentiles
as an outcast, a White, an émigré, a woman
despised for her deep and wayward passion.

Admitted: I have been devoured by life
gathering firewood, feeding my small family.
I have a child who died in an orphanage
(how's that for being "a woman of the age"?)
and I've tried to resurrect my family.
But I've never really cared for "life"—

unmediated, insignificant, all by itself.
Life has to have the plenitude of art.
If I were brought across the sea to Paradise
and forbidden to write, I'd refuse Paradise,
since what good is heaven without art,
which has a joyousness beyond the self?

There are moments in writing like love
when you suddenly set fire to the house
and push your friend from the mountaintop.
They are sublime feelings—the mountaintop
of experience—when you torch the house
and obey the innermost dictates of love.

Wherever you are, I'll reach you, love.
I've named my lust for you "holiness."
We've come to ourselves in a fresh hell
in our century (a godless Russian hell),
but we've also created passionate holiness.
I would be a wing that soars for love.

Oscar Ginsburg

Ladies and Gentlemen, Friends and Strangers:
I stand as a man with spectacles on his nose
(as Isaac Babel said) and autumn in his heart—
a family man, an immigrant, an unknown poet
who scribbles lyrics in the backs of books
about the fair Jerusalem of erotic love.

I never would deliver a commentary on love,
though I affirm its textual strangeness,
a subject taken up by madmen, lovers, poets
who have filled hundreds—thousands—of books
with a Keatsian "holiness of the Heart's
affections," a prayer-book the beloved knows.

Eros is a fiery secret everyone knows
or should know. Cut open my pilgrim heart
and you'll find the sentiments of strangers:
De l'Amour, Liber Amoris,Women in Love,
all the upper registers of romantic poets . . .
(Love, for Jews, is nothing if not bookish.)

A practical woman opened me up like a book
and recited me backwards like a Hebrew poem.
I fell deeply—even desperately—in love
with my wife, a lovely pragmatic stranger
who always wore spectacles on her nose
in matters concerning the human heart.

I speak the backward language of my heart:
"Reprove a man of sense, and he will love
thee" (Proverbs), and she reproved my books,
my airiness, my empty purse which—heaven knows—
I could never fill for my beloved stranger,
who preferred playing cards to reading poems.

And yet Eros is the surest sword of poets—
drawn across beds, cutting through books.
I have known what the migrant heart knows
("O, never say that I was false of heart")
about the steadfast passions of such love
between tender enemies, intimate strangers.

Who knows—but someday the book of my heart
may be inscribed by a stranger, my daughter's
son, brooding about the strangeness of love.

Colette

My mother used to say, "Sit down, dear,
and don't cry. The worst thing for a woman
is her first man—the one who kills you.
After that, marriage becomes a long career."
Poor Sido! She never had another career
and she knew first-hand how love ruins you.
The seducer doesn't care about his woman,
even as he whispers endearments in her ear.

Never let anyone destroy your inner spirit.
Among all the forms of truly absurd courage
the recklessness of young girls is outstanding.
Otherwise there would be far fewer marriages
and even fewer affairs that overwhelm marriages.
Look at me: it's amazing I'm still standing
after what I went through with ridiculous courage.
I was made to suffer, but no one broke my spirit.

Every woman wants her adventure to be a feast
of ripening cherries and peaches, Marseilles figs,
hot-house grapes, champagne shuddering in crystal.
Happiness, we believe, is on sumptuous display.
But unhappiness writes a different kind of play.
The gypsy gazes down into a clear blue crystal
and sees rotten cherries and withered figs.
Trust me: loneliness, too, can be a feast.

Ardor is delicious, but keep your own room.
One of my husbands said: is it impossible
for you to write a book that isn't about love,
adultery, semi-incestuous relations, separation?
(Of course, this was before our own separation.)
He never understood the natural law of love,
the arc from the possible to the impossible . . .
I have extolled the tragedy of the bedroom.

We need exact descriptions of the first passion,
so pay attention to whatever happens to you.
Observe everything: love is greedy and forgetful.
By all means fling yourself wildly into life
(though sometimes you will be flung back by life)
but don't let experience make you forgetful
and be surprised by everything that happens to you.
We are creative creatures fuelled by passion.

One final thought about the nature of love.
Freedom should be the first condition of love
and work is liberating (a novel about love
cannot be written while you are making love).
Never underestimate the mysteries of love,
the eminent dignity of not talking about love.
Passionate attention is prayer, prayer is love.
Savor the world. Consume the feast with love.

From

Lay Back the Darkness

(2003)

I Am Going to Start Living
Like a Mystic

Today I am pulling on a green wool sweater
and walking across the park in a dusky snowfall.

The trees stand like twenty-seven prophets in a field,
each a station in a pilgrimage—silent, pondering.

Blue flakes of light falling across their bodies
are the ciphers of a secret, an occultation.

I will examine their leaves as pages in a text
and consider the bookish pigeons, students of winter.

I will kneel on the track of a vanquished squirrel
and stare into a blank pond for the figure of Sophia.

I shall begin scouring the sky for signs
as if my whole future were constellated upon it.

I will walk home alone with the deep alone,
a disciple of shadows, in praise of the mysteries.

From *The Desire Manuscripts*

The Craving
(*The Odyssey*, Book Twelve)

I needed a warning from the goddess
and a group of men to lash me to the mast
hand and foot, so that I could listen
to swelling, sun-scorched, fatal voices
of two Sirens weaving a haunted sound
over the boiling surf, calling me downward
while I twisted with desire in the ropes
and pleaded to be untied, unbound, unleashed.
How willingly I would have given myself up
to that ardor, that drowning blue charm,
while hopeless clouds scudded overhead
and the deaf oarsmen rowed ruthlessly home.
I was saved, I know, but even now, years later,
I crave those voices dreaming in my sleep.

What the Goddess Can Do
(*The Odyssey,* Book Ten)

Maybe it was the way she held her head
or her voice, which was too high, or her braids,
which reminded me of a girl I used to know,

but I sat on a tall chair like a god
drinking a bowl of honey mulled with wine
and getting drowsy, counting my good fortune,

so that she could transform me into a pig
squealing for acorns, grunting and bristling
in a sty, snouting the ground with other swine.

Later, our leader convinced her to reverse
the spell, setting our animal bodies free . . .

I have been many things in this life —
a husband, a warrior, a seer—but I cannot forget
what the goddess can do to me, if she desires.

The Sentence
(*Inferno,* Canto Five)

When you read Canto Five aloud last night
in your naked, singsong, fractured Italian,
my sweet compulsion, my carnal appetite,

I suspected we shall never be forgiven
for devouring each other body and soul,
and someday Minos, a connoisseur of sin,

will snarl himself twice around his tail
to sentence us to life in perpetual motion,
funneling us downward to the second circle

where we will never sleep or rest again
in turbulent air, like other ill-begotten
lovers who embraced passion beyond reason,

and yet I cannot turn from you, my wanton;
our heaven will always be our hell, a swoon.

In the Mourning Fields
(*The Aeneid,* Book Six)

The world below is starless, stark and deep,
and while you lay beside me, my golden bough,
plunged into the shadowy marsh of sleep,

I read about the infernal realm, and how
a soldier walked forth in the House of Dis
while still alive, breaking an eternal law

by braving death's kingdom, a vast abyss,
the ground sunken in fog—eerie, treacherous—
guarded by a mad beast, three-throated Cerberus.

Tonight I read about us—foundering, hopeless—
in the Mourning Fields and the myrtle grove,
wandering on separate paths, lost in darkness.

It is written that we were consumed by love,
here on earth, a pitiless world above.

The Widening Sky

I am so small walking on the beach
at night under the widening sky.
The wet sand quickens beneath my feet
and the waves thunder against the shore.

I am moving away from the boardwalk
with its colorful streamers of people
and the hotels with their blinking lights.
The wind sighs for hundreds of miles.

I am disappearing so far into the dark
I have vanished from sight.
I am a tiny seashell
that has secretly drifted ashore

and carries the sound of the ocean
surging through its body.
I am so small now no one can see me.
How can I be filled with such a vast love?

My First Theology Lesson

Rumpled and furious, my grandfather's friend
stood up in a bookstore on the North Side
and lamented the lost Jews of Poland

and declared that he felt sorry for God
who had so many problems with Justice
and had become disillusioned and sad

since He wanted to reveal Himself to us
but couldn't find anyone truly worthy
(it was always the wrong time or place

in our deranged and barbaric century)
and so withdrew into His own radiance
and left us a limited mind and body

to contemplate the ghostly absence,
ourselves alone in a divine wilderness.

Lay Back the Darkness

My father in the night shuffling from room to room
on an obscure mission through the hallway.

Help me, spirits, to penetrate his dream
and ease his restless passage.

Lay back the darkness for a salesman
who could charm everything but the shadows,

an immigrant who stands on the threshold
of a vast night

without his walker or his cane
and cannot remember what he meant to say,

though his right arm is raised, as if in prophecy,
while his left shakes uselessly in warning.

My father in the night shuffling from room to room
is no longer a father or a husband or a son,

but a boy standing on the edge of a forest
listening to the distant cry of wolves,

to wild dogs,
to primitive wingbeats shuddering in the treetops.

Yahrzeit Candle

You've lit a candle on the counter between us,
a twenty-four-hour mantra to your mother's passing
from one realm to another twenty years ago,

distillation of grief, wick of suffering,
remembrance of how, after the stark drama
of her last illness, the tragic final act,

we ushered her out of her suburban home
like a pilgrim and handed her over to darkness,
releasing her spirit to the air, a wing,

and turning back to each other in light
of our fresh role as keepers of the dead,
initiates of sorrow, inheritor of prayers,

Lord, which we recite but cannot believe,
grown children swaying to archaic music
and cupping the losses, our bowl of flame.

Dates

I am walking under the palm trees in Miami,
buying a cluster of dates from an Arab vendor.

I want to taste the sweet, sticky flavor of
childhood again, its feathery leaves and secret pits.

My Aunt Lil served dates to our family
in ceramic bowls. She baked them into pastries.

She said that the first taste of a date
is like a child's finger in your mouth,

the second is like the hushed sound
of a father's evening prayer.

———————

The Sufi Master Ibn 'Arabi believed
that God created the palm tree

from the surplus leaven of Adam's clay.
Adam is the origin and archetype

of all human bodies
and the palm, then, is his true sister.

Adam had a sibling rooted to ground
and branching in wind.

For us, therefore, the palm
is like an aunt on our father's side.

———————

The date palm is as vertical as faith—
Ibn 'Arabi compared it to a true believer—

and knows desire. The ancient rabbis spoke
of a female palm outside Tiberias

which withered on its own
and only yielded fruit when pollinated

by a male palm from Jericho.
It thrives in valleys of lowland heat.

My love has moved to the mountains
and I am sending her a palm branch.

———————

There's a victory palm on Hasmonean coins
and Deborah judged her people in the shade

of one as green and fulsome as the Messiah,
a figure, I'm afraid, who does not arrive in time.

The Romans engraved an image
of the captive Judea—*Judea capta*—

sitting in mourning beneath a palm tree,
but I prefer the sturdy angelic palm

I once saw carved on a stone frieze
in a synagogue at Capernaum in Galilee.

———————

When my aunt was too weak to chew,
my cousin mashed a date into puree

and fed it to her with a tiny spoon,
a last honeyed remnant of the garden.

Ibn 'Arabi believed that God laid out
an immense earth from one piece of leaven

the size of a sesame seed.
It was nearly too small to see,

but it unfolded into a world
of plains, mountains, deserts, valleys . . .

———————

The sixth Imam, Ja'far Sadiq, explained
that when God banished Adam

weeping from Paradise
and sheltering a naked wife

He ordered him to uproot the palm
and expel it from the garden

and so Adam replanted it in Mecca.
Thus is the bitter made sweet again.

All other palms, East and West, descend
from pits of those first Medina dates.

———————

My beloved dreamt of a palm tree
buried inside her, and birds singing

canticles of praise day and night.
The birdsong vanished when she woke up

and soon she forgot the enchantment.
All this happened years ago.

But one night when she tasted a date,
she felt a palm spreading its leaves

somewhere inside her
and pure voices rising with wings.

———————

Did I say that the vendor sighed
when he handed me the fleshy fruit?

I wanted the cluster to last
but the sweetness dissolved in my mouth,

which is perishable human clay,
while I strolled under a canopy of trees.

We live on this vast earth for such a short while
that we must mourn and celebrate right now.

A palm leaf is shaped like an open hand.
The taste of dates is holy.

Two Suitcases of Children's Drawings from Terezin, 1942-1944

—In Memory of Friedl Dicker-Brandeis,
Vienna 1898-Auschwitz 1944

1. A Children's Story

Two suitcases sat on a forgotten shelf
collecting dust
            and waited to be remembered

But when the locks were unfastened
the drawings spilled over
                        like a waterfall
and everyone was drenched

2. Artist Unknown

A drawing that looked like the heavens
tilting on one wing

———

A yellow star rising over a blue square

———

A paper cut-out with brown paint
of a man hanging

———

A watercolor on shiny paper
of a girl in pigtails standing with a sword

———

Some wavy green lines on wrapping paper

————————

An unsigned still life with a jelly jar
filled with meadow flowers

————————

A drawing in red pencil of a candlestick

————————

A pasted collage on an office form
of a sunny evening in Terezin

3. What Some of the Class Drew

Zuzga drew the saddest elephant in Block 4

————————

Karel scribbled his name upside down
under a scrawny camel in the desert

————————

Liana painted her face on a tin plate

————————

Franta sketched a sleepy ballerina
lifting her leg over a wooden practice bar

She called it *Memory of a Dancing Girl*

————————

Petr signed his name in the water
that swirled around the deportation train

————————

Soňa crayoned starlight in a dark room

———

František outlined his own hand

———

Mir glued an ambulance from the Red Cross
on semiglossy yellow paper

———

Elly drew a thick diagonal line
but the line needed a partner
and could not live on the paper alone

———

Raja penned an angel with braids
coasting like a hawk over the infirmary

———

Olga created *Paradise with Forbidden Fruit*

———

At twelve
Helga was too old for the children's class
and so she illustrated her father's book

God Came to Terezin and Saw That It Was Bad

4. Children's Voices Spilled out of the Suitcase

This evening we walked along the street of death
we saw them taking away the dead in a wagon

———

189

Don't forget about me
deserted house in the ghetto

———————

We made pets out of our fleas

———————

I couldn't help laughing
when the mustached man with a bald head
checked Mama's head for lice

———————

My suffering took a number

It got in line

———————

We listed all the things we couldn't do
like jumping around on our beds at night
We called the game *No Skipping*

———————

I dreamt my parents got drunk on wine vinegar
and forgot to have me circumcised

———————

Somewhere out there in the trees
far away from the barracks
childhood is still waiting for me

———————

The moon was like a soldier
with a bandaged head

The bandage was soaking wet

_____

The heaviest wheel rolls across our forehead

_____

When you cut the veins of the piano
and let the blood flow through the notes
grief had a new name

_____

Your eyes were as dark as skullcaps

Your forehead was as heavy as the heavens before it rains

_____

Papa was one of the skeletons
harnessed to a funeral cart
carrying bread to the canteen

_____

To make me laugh
the man with a long beard
wriggled his eyebrows

_____

Hunger drained the last grays from his face

_____

The yellow dandelions flew around our heads
like butterflies

_____

Butterflies vanished

This is a guard with a stick

This is a stick with a heart

This is a heart with a horseshoe

This is a girl flinging the horseshoe
at a guard

_____

The boy drew a suitcase on scrap paper

He folded the paper and put it in a suitcase

He left the suitcase open in the rain

_____

All night the girl looked out the window
until the window disappeared
and there was no girl

_____

The simple son was pulverized
by the back of a rifle

The wise son forgot to ask

_____

We disliked the ancient story
of the sacrificial lamb
who wandered into a slaughteryard

and yet no one revised it

———

No one in dormitory L410 remembered
if the Talmud was written
in black letters on white fire
or in white letters on black fire

———

Some people despise the color green
because it is the offspring
of a mixed marriage
between celestial blue and earthly yellow

———

Someone was always shouting at us
in a language we didn't understand

The Tower of Babel had become a pit

———

She painted herself light blue
when she felt like a flute

She painted herself dark blue
when she felt like a cello

She painted herself black and blue
when she was bruised into silence

———

He drew a German shepherd inside a cage
and blackened the cage with a crayon

It was sealed shut
but he could hear the dog barking at night

————

The passive element of the blue in red
could still make her sad

and the purple light sinking to black
echoed a grief that was scarcely human

————

We did not make graven images
we made images from the grave

————

Not even the teacher
who studied at the Bauhaus
could draw the face of God

————

The Rabbi said that Adonai
hides in the Hebrew alphabet
but we didn't know Hebrew
and we didn't believe him

————

Someone wrote in tiny letters in pencil

I don't believe God forgot us

but someone else scrawled in thick letters in pen

I don't believe

God forgot us

6. The Art Teacher

Frau Brandeis said that every object tells a story
if you look hard

She said that art supplies perspective
and engraves memories

She said that childhood is genius

and she praised her teachers who believed
in seven axioms

Force   Intensity   Form   Dimension
Character   Composition   Color

She believed in mixing pigments
and drawing from nature

She taught exercises in composition
and breathing

She spoke of positive and negative forms
and the rhythm of geometric shapes
and the musical keyboard of color

Often we drew with charcoal
to the colorful sound of her voice

She said that we are like mortar
or stone in a fresh building

She told us to imagine ourselves
as an open window or a rising staircase
or a bamboo tree growing in bursts

She said something about the emancipated line
and the aspirations of the vertical

She praised the illuminating hand

Light absorbed her

————

It still seemed natural for her
to pass around pencils and paper

She said
        The wisdom lives in the pencil
and the paper remembers everything

————

But no one drew pictures anymore
after the materials ran out

and the art teacher
was deported

7. Art Project

Cut 15,000 pieces of paper into dolls
Each piece of paper represents one child

Now start a bonfire
and burn 14,900 of the paper dolls

Keep 100

8. The Angel of Mercy
did not get up

It did not unleash our thirty thousand wings

——— —

Smoke from the oncoming trains blackened our faces

———

Fog invaded the camp

The sky was like a blackboard
clouded with erasures

———

The coward moon cowered in the clouds

———

The city spires pretended to be asleep

Stars muffled their lights

———

The sun at night witnessed everything
from a secret place behind the bridge
but it was too frightened to rise

———————

All the transports headed east into nothingness

———————

Brushes forgot themselves

Pencils expired

———————

Someone stuffed the drawings into two suitcases

———————

The drawings whispered like secrets in the dark

———————

The secrets were a children's story

———————

The story waited patiently to be told

———————

Two suitcases sat on a forgotten shelf
collecting dust

9. The Injunction

At the end of the story
the locks were fastened again

The new teacher shut the school
and went home

But the waterfall did not stop
and the magic suitcases could not be closed

The injunction was scribbled in a child's hand

Whoever looks at these drawings
shall stand under the waterfall
                    and remember

10. Far Away

Somewhere a blue horse floats
over a sloping roof

and a kite soars away from its string

From *The Hades Sonnets*

The Forgetfulness Chair

My obstinate, self-absorbed, courageous
father, shuffling across the living room floor
to the determined chair in the far corner,

where my mother covered him with a blanket
and he promptly dozed off and woke up
later without knowing where he'd awakened,

was Peirithoüs slipping into the under-
world through the open gate at Taenarum
to abduct Persephone, the queen of death,

while Hades, the Unseen One, coaxed him
into sitting down on the chair of Lethe,
the stony black seat of Forgetfulness,

where he forgot why he had entered Hell
and never found his way back to the living.

The Asphodel Meadows

I dreamt that I found our bloodless Shades
moving among the less distinguished dead
in the Asphodel Meadows, a realm of Hades

reserved for those who are neither good
nor evil, for souls without purpose,
and I poured out libations of blood

before I turned in a fury on Minos
and raged about the past we had suffered
together, our quirky moments of grace,

the loved ones, the deaths we had tended,
the work we had made, the desperate charms
we had uttered on behalf of our child,

but the god was indifferent to our terms,
and then I woke with you in my arms.

Self-portrait as Eurydice

How I dreamt about your engulfing arms,
my Orphic secret, my haunting primal chant,
from my place amid the phantom forms

and waited for you to startle the grave
path into the underworld—dank, silent—
where I shivered in the night's embrace

until I heard your fatal cry, your fate-
ful voice rising like a forgotten dream
or a wandering soul calling for light

in eternity's dense fog, an eager song,
and I followed it toward the earth's seam
hoping to breathe again, listening,

until you whirled around, my dark flame,
and then I died for you a second time.

Self-portrait as Hades
and Persephone

Out of the nether regions of nightfall
in a spectral valley, the House of Dis,
out of the smoky river and black tunnel,

I suddenly recognized myself as Hades
devouring the maidenhead, a fresh girl
staring into the yellow eye of narcissus,

an amorous innocent, a wide-eyed pupil
I also recognized as some part of my-
self ravenous to experience Hell,

eager for dark knowledge of the body,
the long night of the descending soul,
the madness beneath the surface of day,

and so I married myself to a cycle
that was demonic, treacherous, immortal.

From

Special Orders

(2008)

Special Orders

Give me back my father walking the halls
    of Wertheimer Box and Paper Company
        with sawdust clinging to his shoes.

Give me back his tape measure and his keys,
    his drafting pencil and his order forms;
        give me his daydreams on lined paper.

I don't understand this uncontainable grief.
    Whatever you had that never fit,
        whatever else you needed, believe me,

my father, who wanted your business,
    would squat down at your side
        and sketch you a container for it.

Cotton Candy

We walked on the bridge over the Chicago River
for what turned out to be the last time,
and I ate cotton candy, that sugary air,
that sweet blue light spun out of nothingness.
It was just a moment, really, nothing more,
but I remember marveling at the sturdy cables
of the bridge that held us up
and threading my fingers through the long
and slender fingers of my grandfather,
an old man from the Old World
who long ago disappeared into the nether regions.
And I remember that eight-year-old boy
who had tasted the sweetness of air,
which still clings to my mouth
and disappears when I breathe.

Branch Library

I wish I could find that skinny, long-beaked boy
who perched in the branches of the old branch library.

He spent the Sabbath flying between the wobbly stacks
and the flimsy wooden tables on the second floor,

pecking at nuts, nesting in broken spines, scratching
notes under his own corner patch of sky.

I'd give anything to find that birdy boy again
bursting out into the dusky blue afternoon

with his satchel of scrawls and scribbles,
radiating heat, singing with joy.

Playing the Odds

The Vegas lights are glaring at one a.m.
and I can still see my bulky first father
standing at the craps table
whispering softly to the dice,
Come on, baby, come home to Daddy.

He is surrounded by strangers who are
shouting out numbers, laying down bets,
and he is massively alone, like God
playing dice with the universe
on a felt table in a fake city.

My sister and I watch him from the crowd.
Our father wants a seven coming out.
He wants to roll dice until he can't win
anymore, and then he needs to lose.
But everyone likes him for that seven.

I was two years old when I last saw him
blowing on the dice in our kitchen.
These are the true numbers, he said,
cupping them in his palms,
and then he tossed them on the table.

I remember the sweaty warmth
of those dice before he threw them.
I wonder if God Himself
breathed into the nostrils of His son
with as much tenderness and desperation.

—For Harold Rubenstein, 1928-2004

The Chardin Exhibition

—For William Maxwell

While I was studying the copper cistern
and the silver goblet, a soup tureen
with a cat stalking a partridge and hare,

you were gulping down the morning light
and moving from the bedstand to the bureau,
from the shuttered window to the open door.

While I was taking my time over a pristine jar
of apricots and a basket of wild strawberries—
a pyramid leaning toward a faceted glass—

you were sitting at a low breakfast table
eating a soft-boiled egg—just one—
from a tiny, hesitant, glittering spoon.

While I was absorbed in a duck hanging
by one leg and a hare with a powder flask
and a game bag, which you wanted me to see,

you were lying on the living room couch
for a nap, one of your last, next to
a white porcelain vase with two carnations.

I wish I could have stood there with you
in front of Chardin's last self-portrait,
exclaiming over his turban with a bow

and the red splash of his pastel crayon—
a new medium—which he used, dearest,
to defy death on a sheet of blue paper.

Kraków, Six A.M.

—For Adam Zagajewski

I sit in a corner of the town square
and let the ancient city move through me.
I sip a cup of coffee, write a little,
and watch an old woman sweeping the stairs.

Poland is waking up now: blackbirds patrol
the cobblestones, nuns rush by in habits,
and the clock tower strikes six times.
Day breaks into the night's reverie.

The morning is as fresh and clean
as a butcher's apron hanging in a shop.
Now it is pressed and white, but soon
it will be spotted with blood.

Europe is waking up, but America
is going to sleep, a gangly teenager
sprawled out on a comfortable bed.
He has large hands and feet

and his dreams are innocent and bloodthirsty.
I want to throw a blanket over his shoulders
and tuck him in again, like a child,
now that his sleep is no longer untroubled.

I'm alone here in the Old World
where poetry matters, old hatreds seethe,

and history wears a crown of thorns.
Fresh bread wafts from the ovens

and daily life follows its own inexorable
course, like a drunk weaving slowly
across a courtyard, or a Dutch maid
throwing open the heavy shutters.

I suppose there's always a shopgirl
stationed in the doorway, a beggar taking up
his corner post, and newspapers fluttering
from store to store with bad news.

Poetry, too, seeks a place in the world—
feasting on darkness but needing light,
taking confession, listening for bells,
for the first strains of music in a town square.

Europe is going to work now—
look at those two businessmen hurrying
past the statue of the national bard—
as her younger brother sleeps

on the other side of the ocean,
innocent and violent, dreaming of glory.

Elegy for the Jewish Villages

—After Antoni Słonimsky

The Jewish villages in Poland are gone now—
Hrubieszów, Karczew, Brody, Falenica . . .
There are no Sabbath candles lit in the windows,
no chanting comes from the wooden synagogues.

The Jewish villages in Poland have vanished
and so I walked through a graveyard without graves.
It must have been hard work to clean up after the war:
someone must have sprinkled sand over the blood,
swept away the footprints, and whitewashed the walls
with bluish lime. Someone must have fumigated
the streets, the way you do after a plague.

One moon glitters here—cold, pale, alien.
I stood in the dark countryside in summer but
could never find the two golden moons of Chagall
glittering outside the town when the night lights up.
Those moons are orbiting another planet now.

Gone are the towns where the shoemaker was a poet,
the watchmaker a philosopher, the barber a troubadour.

Gone are the villages where the wind joined biblical songs
with Polish tunes, where old Jews stood in the shade
of cherry trees and longed for the holy walls of Jerusalem.

Gone now are the hamlets that passed away
like a shadow that falls between our words.

I am bringing you home the story of a world—
Hrubieszów, Karczew, Brody, Falenica . . .
Come close and listen to this song—
the Jewish villages in Poland are gone now—
from another one of the saddest nations on earth.

The Minimalist Museum

I am driving past our house on Sul Ross
across the street from the minimalist museum.

I am looking up at the second-story window
where I gazed down at the curators

carrying their leather satchels to work
and the schoolchildren gathering on the front lawn.

I spent my forties at that window, stirring milk
into my coffee and brooding about the past,

listening to Satie's experiments and Cage's
dicey music wafting over the temple of modernism.

I chanced a decade at that window, impervious
to the precarious moment, the broken moon-

light flooding over the neighborhood trees,
my wife's moody insomnia, my son's fitful sleep,

and sacrificing another five years, another ten years,
to the minor triumphs, the major failures.

Self-portrait

I lived between my heart and my head,
like a married couple who can't get along.

I lived between my left arm, which is swift
and sinister, and my right, which is righteous.

I lived between a laugh and a scowl,
and voted against myself, a two-party system.

My left leg dawdled or danced along,
my right cleaved to the straight and narrow.

My left shoulder was like a stripper on vacation,
my right stood upright as a Roman soldier.

Let's just say that my left side was the organ
donor and leave my private parts alone,

but as for my eyes, which are two shades
of brown, well, Dionysus, meet Apollo.

Look at Eve raising her left eyebrow
while Adam puts his right foot down.

No one expected it to survive,
but divorce seemed out of the question.

I suppose my left hand and my right hand
will be clasped over my chest in the coffin

and I'll be reconciled at last,
I'll be whole again.

A Partial History of My Stupidity

Traffic was heavy coming off the bridge,
and I took the road to the right, the wrong one,
and got stuck in the car for hours.

Most nights I rushed out into the evening
without paying attention to the trees,
whose names I didn't know,
or the birds, which flew heedlessly on.

I couldn't relinquish my desires
or accept them, and so I strolled along
like a tiger that wanted to spring
but was still afraid of the wildness within.

The iron bars seemed invisible to others,
but I carried a cage around inside me.

I cared too much what other people thought
and made remarks I shouldn't have made.
I was silent when I should have spoken.

Forgive me, philosophers,
I read the Stoics but never understood them.

I felt that I was living the wrong life,
spiritually speaking,
while halfway around the world

thousands of people were being slaughtered,
some of them by my countrymen.

So I walked on—distracted, lost in thought—
and forgot to attend to those who suffered
far away, nearby.

Forgive me, faith, for never having any.

I did not believe in God,
who eluded me.

Late March

Saturday morning in late March.
I was alone and took a long walk,
though I also carried a book
of the Alone, which companioned me.

The day was clear, unnaturally clear,
like a freshly wiped pane of glass,
a window over the water,
and blue, preternaturally blue,
like the sky in a Magritte painting,
and cold, vividly cold, so that
you could clap your hands and remember
winter, which had left a few moments ago—
if you strained, you could almost see it
disappearing over the hills in a black parka.
Spring was coming but hadn't arrived yet.
I walked on the edge of the park.
The wind whispered a secret to the trees,
which held their breath
and scarcely moved.
On the other side of the street,
the skyscrapers stood on tiptoe.

I walked down to the pier to watch
the launching of a passenger ship.
Ice had broken up on the river
and the water rippled smoothly in blue light.
The moon was a faint smudge

in the clouds, a brushstroke, an afterthought
in the vacant mind of the sky.
Seagulls materialized out of vapor
amidst the masts and flags.
Don't let our voices die on land,
they cawed, swooping down for fish
and then soaring back upwards.

The kiosks were opening
and couples moved slowly past them,
arm in arm, festive.
Children darted in and out of walkways,
which sprouted with vendors.
Voices cut the air.
Kites and balloons. Handmade signs.
Voyages to unknown places.
The whole day had the drama of an expectation.

Down at the water, the queenly ship
started moving away from the pier.
Banners fluttered.
The passengers clustered at the rails on deck.
I stood with the people onshore and waved
goodbye to the travelers.
Some were jubilant;
others were brokenhearted.
I have always been both.

Suddenly, a great cry went up.
The ship set sail for the horizon
and rumbled into the future,

but the cry persisted
and cut the air
like an iron bell ringing
in an empty church.
I looked around the pier,
but everyone else was gone
and I was left alone
to peer into the ghostly distance.
I had no idea where that ship was going,
but I felt lucky to see it off
and bereft when it disappeared.

To D. B.

I miss your apartment on West Eleventh Street
where I slept off the front hall in a bedroom
that would have been a closet in another city.

The plants breathed easily in their heavy pots,
but the radiators knocked all night, like ghosts
trying to reach us from the other side.

The traffic on Sixth Avenue was a slow buzz.
Someone rattled a dog chain in the moonlight
that bathed the schoolyard across the street.

Light seeped in through the barred windows.
I could hear Faith rustling around downstairs,
getting ready for work, unwilling to die.

If there is a West Village in the other world,
we will someday meet there. I'll reach over
and hug you, which will make you uneasy.

Let's go for a bottle of wine at the tavern
near the branch library and then stroll over
to Citarella for prosciutto and melon.

You can buy a pack of cigarettes at the corner
and explain the architecture to me. Maybe
I can stay at your place until I get settled.

Boy with a Headset

He is wearing baggy shorts and a loud T-shirt
and singing along to his headset on Broadway.
Every now and then he glances back at me,
a middle-aged father weaving through traffic behind him.

He is a fifteen-year-old in the city—no more, no less—
but I imagine him as a colorful unnamed bird
warbling his difference from the robins and sparrows
and scissoring past the vendors on every corner.

I keep thinking of him as a wild fledgling
who tilts precariously on one wing
and peers back at me from the sudden height
before sailing out over the treetops.

Green Figs

I want to live like that little fig tree
   that sprouted up at the beach last spring
      and spread its leaves over the sandy rock.

All summer its stubborn green fruit
   (tiny flowers covered with a soft skin)
      ripened and grew in the bright salt spray.

The Tree of the Knowledge of Good
   and Evil was a fig tree, or so it is said,
      but this wild figure was a wanton stray.

I need to live like that crooked tree—
   solitary, bittersweet, and utterly free—
      that knelt down in the hardest winds

but could not be blasted away.
   It kept its eye on the far horizon
      and brought honey out of the rock.

The Sweetness

Tornami avanti, s'alcun dolce mai ebbe 'l cor tristo . . .

—PETRARCH, #272

The times my sad heart knew a little sweetness
come back to me now: the coffee shop
in Decatur, the waffle house in Macon . . .

The highway signs pointed to our happiness;
the greasy spoons and gleaming truck stops
were the stations of our pilgrimage.

Remember the flock of Baptist women flying
off the bus and gathering on the bridge
over the river, singing with praise?

Wasn't that us staggering past the riverboats,
eating homemade fudge at the county fair
and devouring each other's body?

They come back to me now, delicious love,
the times my sad heart knew a little sweetness.

A New Theology

God couldn't bear their happiness
when He heard them laughing together in the garden.
He caught them kneeling down in the dirt
(or worse) and letting pomegranate juice
run down their faces. He found them
breaking open a fig with fresh delight
as if something crucial had dawned upon them.
I think the whole shebang—the serpent, the apple
with knowledge of good and evil—was a setup
because God couldn't stand being alone
with His own creation, while Adam and Eve celebrated
as a man and a woman together in Paradise,
exactly like us, love, exactly like us.

I Wish I Could Paint You

I wish I could paint you—
your lanky body, lithe, coltish, direct.
I need a brush for your hard angles
and ferocious blues and reds.
I need to stretch a fresh canvas
to catch you stretched across the bed.

I wish I could paint you
from the waist up—your gangling arms
and flat chest, your long neck
(it would take Modigliani to capture it)
that has caused you so much pain
holding up your proud head.

I wish I could paint you
from the waist down—your cheeky
ass, your cunt like the steely eye
of a warrior queen, your tall
thoroughbred legs— headlong, furious- -
that have ridden me to victory.

I watch you sleeping next to me
in a patch of light, or stepping out
of the shower in the early morning,
your smile as wide as the sea
and your eyes that are deeper blue.
I wish I could paint you.

To the Subway

Underground horse, I board you at Grand Central
and ride your steely body away from the city
with the other riders, the collared and collarless.

I prefer you expressly, at off-hours,
but I hang from your bars at peak times
and sway to your snorting music.

I lean in to your turns in dank tunnels
and hurtle with you through the darkness
for long stretches, between fitful stops.

I'm not pretending I never curse you
for rearing up between stations, breaking down
on Thursdays, or resting in your stable,

and yet you carry me faithfully to Atlantic
where I step across the gap onto firm shore
and climb your stairs into the bright air.

Green Couch

That was the year I lived without fiction
and slept surrounded by books on the unconscious.
I woke every morning to a sturdy brown oak.

That was the year I left behind my marriage
of twenty-eight years, my faded philosophy books, and
the green couch I had inherited from my grandmother.

After she died, I drove it across the country
and carried it up three flights of crooked stairs
to a tiny apartment in West Philadelphia,

and stored it in my in-laws' basement in Bethesda,
and left it to molder in our garage in Detroit
(my friend Dennis rescued it for his living room),

and moved it to a second-floor study in Houston
and a fifth-floor apartment on the Upper West Side,
where it will now be carted away to the dump.

All my difficult reading took place on that couch,
which was turning back into the color of nature
while I grappled with ethics and the law,

the reasons for Reason, Being and Nothingness,
existential dread and the death of God
(I'm still angry at Him for no longer existing).

That was the year when I finally mourned
for my two dead fathers, my sole marriage,
and the electric green couch of my past.

Darlings, I remember everything.
But now I try to speak the language of
the unconscious and study earth for secrets.

I go back and forth to work.
I walk in the botanical gardens on weekends
and take a narrow green path to the clearing.

After a Long Insomniac Night

I walked down to the sea in the early morning
after a long insomniac night.

I climbed over the giant gull-colored rocks
and moved past the trees,
tall dancers stretching their limbs
and warming up in the blue light.

I entered the salty water, a penitent
whose body was stained,
and swam toward a red star rising
in the east—regal, purple-robed.

One shore disappeared behind me
and another beckoned.
                    I confess
that I forgot the person I had been
as easily as the clouds drifting overhead.

My hands parted the water.
The wind pressed at my back, wings
and my soul floated over the whitecapped waves.

Acknowledgments

I am deeply grateful to my three splendid poetry editors at Knopf
who have sustained me through the years: Alice Quinn,
Harry Ford, and Deborah Garrison.

Special thanks to the editors of the following publications where the
new poems in this book, some of which have been revised, first appeared:

The American Poetry Review: "The Beginning of Poetry," "Isis Unveiled,"
"Winter in Edinburgh," "Once, in Helsinki," "The Case Against Poetry,"
"Milk," "What the Last Evening Will Be Like"

Callaloo: "Anything but Standard"

Five Points: "Dark Tour," "Last Saturday," "Forebodings"

The New York Review of Books: "On the Anniversary of Joseph Brodsky's Death"

Northwest Review: "Early Sunday Morning"

237

A Note About the Author

Edward Hirsch is the author of seven previous collections of poetry, including *Wild Gratitude,* which won the National Book Critics Circle Award, and *Special Orders.* He has also published four prose books, among them *How to Read a Poem and Fall in Love with Poetry,* a national best seller. He has received numerous awards for his poetry, including a MacArthur Fellowship, and publishes regularly in a wide variety of magazines and journals, including *American Poetry Review* and *The New Yorker.* A longtime teacher in the Creative Writing Program at the University of Houston, he is now the president of the John Simon Guggenheim Memorial Foundation.

A Note on the Type

The text of this book was set in a typeface named Perpetua, designed by the British artist Eric Gill (1882–1940) and cut by the Monotype Corporation of London in 1928–30. Perpetua is a contemporary letter of original design, without any direct historical antecedents. The shapes of the roman letters basically derive from stonecutting, a form of lettering in which Gill was eminent. The italic is essentially an inclined roman. The general effect of the typeface in reading sizes is one of lightness and grace.

COMPOSED BY
North Market Street Graphics, Lancaster, Pennsylvania

PRINTED AND BOUND BY
Thomson-Shore, Inc., Dexter, Michigan

DESIGNED BY
Iris Weinstein